Information Science

THE STUDY OF SCIENCE

Information Science

Edited by Mary Lee Balice

Britannica Educational Publishing

IN ASSOCIATION WITH

ROSEN EDUCATIONAL SERVICES

Published in 2017 by Britannica Educational Publishing (a trademark of Encyclopædia Britannica, Inc.)
in association with The Rosen Publishing Group, Inc.
29 East 21st Street, New York, NY 10010

Distributed exclusively by Rosen Publishing.
To see additional Britannica Educational Publishing titles, go to rosenpublishing.com.

First Edition

Britannica Educational Publishing
J.E. Luebering: Director, Core Reference Group
Anthony L. Green: Editor, Compton's by Britannica

Rosen Publishing
Kathy Kuhtz Campbell: Senior Editor
Nelson Sá: Art Director
Brian Garvey: Designer
Cindy Reiman: Photography Manager
Karen Huang: Photo Researcher
Supplementary material by Mary Lee Balice

Library of Cataloging-in-Publication Data

Names: Balice, Mary Lee, editor.
Title: Information science / edited by Mary Lee Balice.
Description: New York, NY : Britannica Educational Publishing in Association with Rosen Educational Services, 2017. | Series: The study of science | Audience: Grades 7 to 12. | Includes bibliographical references and index.
Identifiers: LCCN 2015035842 | ISBN 9781680482324 (library bound)
Subjects: LCSH: Information science--Juvenile literature. | Information resources management--Juvenile literature. | Information science libraries--Juvenile literature.
Classification: LCC Z665.5 .I54 2016 | DDC 020--dc23
LC record available at http://lccn.loc.gov/2015035842

Manufactured in China

Photo credits:
Cover, p. 3 Sergey Nivens/Shutterstock.com; pp. 8–9 Miami Herald/Tribune News Service/Getty Images; pp. 14–15, 21, 26 (recreated), 48 (recreated), 66 (recreated), 67 (recreated), 75 (recreated) Encyclopaedia Britannica, Inc.; p. 17 Cloyd Teter/Denver Post/Getty Images; p. 18 Johan Swanepoel/Shutterstock.com; p. 29 BSIP/Universal Images Group/Getty Images; p. 37 Keystone-France/Gamma-Keystone/Getty Images; p. 41 cristi180884/Shutterstock.com; p. 45 yurchello108/Shutterstock.com; p. 53 © Mary Evans Picture Library/Alamy; p. 87 ColorBlind Images/Iconica/Getty Images; p. 88 Jason Doiy/E+/Getty Images; p. 101 DEA/G. Dagli Orti/De Agostini/Getty Images; p. 102 Science and Society/SuperStock; p. 105 Comstock/Stockbyte/Thinkstock; p. 106 © Rob/Alamy; p. 108 Thomas Northcut/Photodisc/Thinkstock; p. 111 dotshock/Shutterstock.com; pp. 115, 117 © AP Images; p. 125 Fuse/Getty Images; cover and interior pages backgrounds and borders © iStockphoto.com/LuMaxArt.

CONTENTS

INTRODUCTION

Using a laptop, a college mentor helps a high school student retrieve information during a research project at the Miami-Dade Public Library.

Information science deals with the processes of storing and transferring information. It attempts to bring together concepts and methods from various disciplines such as library science, computer science and engineering, linguistics, psychology, and other technologies to develop techniques and devices to aid in the handling of information. Information science, sometimes called informatics, is concerned with thc collcction, organization, storage, retrieval, interpretation, and use of information.

The transfer of information through time requires the existence of some storage medium, which is designated a document—hence the term "documentation." Historically documentation emerged as a distinct discipline in the early 20th century, paralleling the rise of empirical research (that is, research based on observation or experience), which was to provide its main source of subjects. Documentation as a discipline flourished in response to the growth of the periodical and the journal as the primary media for scientific reports. Whereas books required control through cataloging and classification, periodicals required indexes and abstracts that would bring together for the researcher primary information originally published in different sources.

The roots of information science lay in three post-World War II developments: development of a key information-theory model, an early conception of the science of cybernetics, and rapid advances in the design and production of electronic computers. These innovations pointed to a new field of study in which many disciplines could be merged under the unifying idea of "information." After the Georgia Institute of Technology established the first formal information science program in 1963, the discipline quickly developed at a number of other universities either as an independent field of study or as a specialty within such departments as library science, computer science, or engineering.

In its early stages during the 1960s, information science was primarily concerned with applying the then-new computer technology to the processing and managing of documents. Modeling studies were undertaken on various concepts, including the effectiveness of information storage and retrieval, various modes of human-machine interaction, and the effect of form on the content and comprehension of information.

The applied computer technologies—and more recently, the theoretical areas of study—of information science have since spread throughout many other disciplines and have even been appropriated by new fields. Computer science and engineering tend to focus on theory and technology-oriented subjects, whereas management science tends to absorb subjects directly related to information systems. There are hundreds of professional associations that are concerned with information-related disciplines, providing a forum where people can exchange ideas about information processing.

In *Information Science*, readers will discover how disciplines, concepts, and digital technologies intertwine and how people use them to share information or data. The foremost concept of information science is information—its verbal, visual, and quantitative arrangements—and how that information (including mobile information) is stored, studied, examined, processed, and communicated by machines and society.

CHAPTER 1

INFORMATION THEORY

The era we are living in is sometimes called the age of information. But what is information, and how much of it is in any message? Let's look at two situations to determine their information content. Suppose you planned to play tennis with a friend at a nearby park but a heavy rain prevents you from leaving the house. Then the telephone rings and your friend tells you the game is off because it is raining. This message holds no information because you already know it is raining. Suppose, however, that you planned to play at a park by your friend's house several miles away, the sky was overcast, and the weatherman the night before had said that the chance of rain in the morning was high. Then your friend calls and says the game is off because it is raining there. This message contains information because prior to receiving it you were not certain whether it was raining at the park. Information, therefore, is anything that resolves uncertainty.

Information theory measures information. It also investigates the efficient use of information media. A system of information communication is composed of several components. First, the information source produces the message, or information, to be transmitted. Next, the encoder, or transmitter, processes the message and changes it to a signal suitable for the channel. (The channel is the medium over which the signal is sent. Random disturbances, or noise, on the channel cause the received signal to be somewhat different from the transmitted one. Noise imposes serious limitations on the amount of information that can be transmitted over a channel.) Finally, the decoder, or receiver, processes the received signal to recreate the original message.

Block Diagram of a Communication System

The block diagram illustrates these components by using the key events of Paul Revere's famed midnight ride in 1775 to warn colonial patriots northwest of Boston of an impending British raid. The information source was the British army, and the source output was the information whether the British troops would attack the Massachusetts towns of Lexington and Concord by land or by sea. The encoder/transmitter was the sexton of the North Church who was to place one lantern in the belfry to indicate attack by land or two lanterns for attack by sea. The channel was the line of sight from the belfry to the place where Paul Revere, the decoder/receiver, was waiting. Anything that obstructed Revere's view, such as wind-tossed tree branches, created noise. The communication was only a selection between two alternatives—attack by land or attack by sea. As long as prior agreement existed between

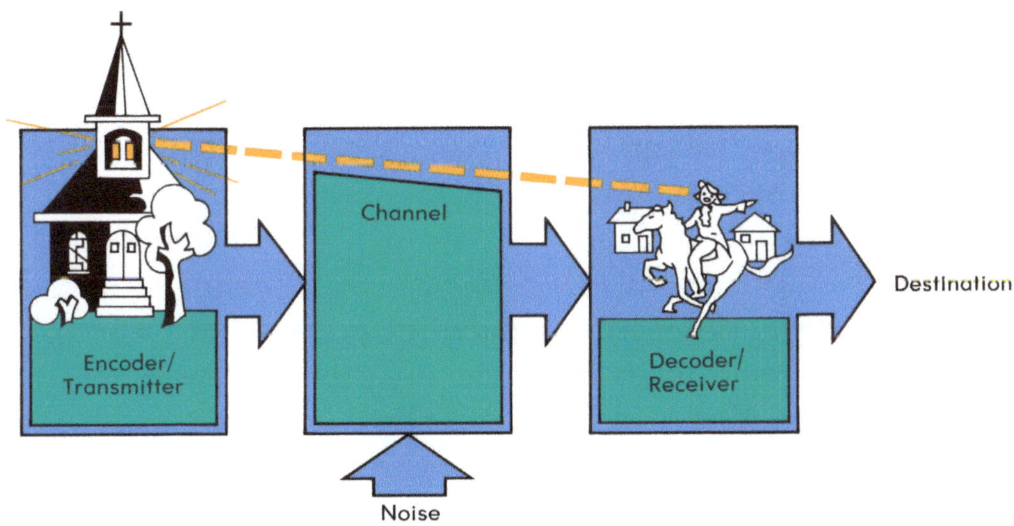

A block diagram depicts the concept of a communication system in information theory.

encoder and decoder (the sexton and Revere) on the alternatives and their proper signals, this communication system could have sent a selection from any set of two alternatives. For example, were they infantry or artillery troops? A more complex system would have been needed to communicate the number of troops in the raid because of the larger number of possible alternatives.

Binary Digits and Information Transmission

Teletype communication offers a good example of information transmission. In teletype communication the source is the person operating a teletypewriter, an instrument that transmits and receives messages via telephone cables or radio relay systems. The teletypewriter, in turn, is the encoder. The machine is connected by telephone wire (the channel) to a teleprinter (the decoder) in a distant city. The person sends a message by pressing down on the teletypewriter keys. Those keys are a set of alternatives. The pressing of each key triggers transmission of a sequence of binary digits that represent the letter on that key. A binary digit is either a 0 or a 1. From the teletypewriter

Information transmission can be represented by teletype communication. A person at the keyboard is the source; the machine is the transmitter, receiver, and encoder; and the telephone wire is the channel to the teleprinter, or the decoder.

pulsating information encoded in binary digits is sent over commercial telephone lines. At the other end, the sequence of binary digits is decoded back to the appropriate letters. Binary digits underlie the language of computers.

For information theory purposes, the length of the binary sequence needed for encoding individual letters is more important than how the teletypewriter actually encodes the information. Only two binary digits are needed to represent four alternatives—00, 01, 10, and 11. Similarly, three binary digits can represent

This photograph shows an example of binary code. A binary code is a code used in computers, based on a binary number system, and involves a method of calculating and representing information by using the numbers 0 and 1.

eight alternatives—000, 001, 010, 011, 100, 101, 110, and 111. As a general principle, each increase of one in the sequence length doubles the number of alternatives (2 binary digits—4 alternatives, 3—8, 4—16, and so on). In mathematical shorthand, we can say a sequence of *n* binary digits can represent 2^n alternatives.

Logarithms, especially base-two logarithms (log_2), are used in the computation of information content. The base-two logarithm of a number is defined as the power to which two must be raised in order to get that number; hence, for any number n, $\log_2(2^n) = n$. As a result, if a teletypewriter has m keys on its keyboard, any individual key must activate a sequence of binary digits that is at least $\log_2 m$ long. For example, if a keyboard holds 32 keys, a sequence of five binary digits can represent any given key (00000 for A, 00001 for B, and so on) because the base-two logarithm of 32 is 5.00000.

Human communication is still another example of information transmission. A person with an idea is the source, and the idea is the source output. The idea is encoded into words and written. Another person decodes the words when reading them and tries to reconstruct the writer's idea. Each written word was selected from a set of alternatives—that is, all the words of the language. Information theory has not shed much light on biological communication because living communication systems are not well enough understood for the application of the mathematical concepts of the theory. However, the basic notion of information as a transmission of binary digits that represents a choice from a set of alternatives should prove helpful in future research into biological information systems.

Claude Shannon (1916–2001)

American engineer Claude Shannon's master's thesis, "A Symbolic Analysis of Relay and Switching Circuits" (1940), established the theoretical underpinnings of digital circuits. Digital circuits are fundamental to the operation of modern computers and telecommunications equipment, making Shannon's dissertation one of the most significant theses of the 20th century.

Shannon's 1948 paper "A Mathematical Theory of Communication" built on the foundations of other researchers at Bell Labs, such as Harry Nyquist and R.V.L. Hartley. Shannon's paper, however, went far beyond the earlier work. It established the basic results of information theory in such a complete form that his framework and terminology are still used.

Shannon separated the technical problem of delivering a message from the problem of understanding what a message means. He focused on two key concerns: determining the most efficient encoding of a message using a given alphabet in a noiseless environment, and understanding what additional steps need to be taken in the presence of noise.

Shannon solved these problems successfully for a widely applicable model of a communications system that includes both discrete (digital) and continuous (analog) systems. His contributions to information theory were an immediate success with communications engineers and continue to prove useful. Shannon's work inspired many attempts to apply information theory in other areas, such as biology, linguistics, psychology, economics, and physics.

Renowned for his eclectic interests and capabilities—including such activities as juggling while riding a unicycle down the halls of Bell Labs—Shannon produced

many provocative and influential articles on information theory, cryptography, and chess-playing computers, as well as designing various mechanical devices.

CHANNELS AND NOISE

Whether the channel of an information system is a wire, a radio wavelength, a laser beam, or some other medium, the output signal of the system is never quite the same as the

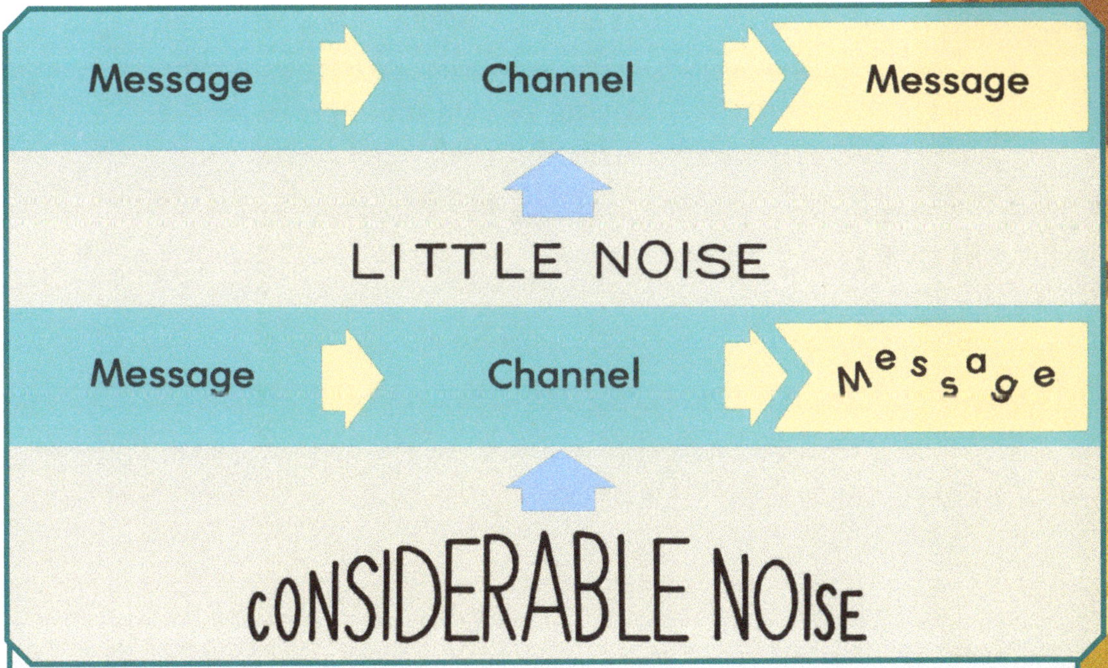

When great enough, random disturbances called noise can garble or distort a message being transmitted over a channel.

input signal because of noise intruding on the channel. Noise can be caused by heat, atmospheric disturbances, or cross talk, which is a form of interference from other channels. Static in a radio, snow on a television screen, and background hum in a telephone are familiar examples of noise. To send information over radio, television, and telephone channels, a modem system (digital data *mo*dulator and *dem*odulator) must be used. At one end of the channel the modulator converts the sequence of symbols making up the information into a signal suitable for transmission over the channel. At the other end the demodulator changes the received signal back into the original sequence of symbols. Noise, however, interferes by causing occasional errors at the receiving end of the channel.

CHAPTER 2

INFORMATION PROCESSING: AN OVERVIEW

Information processing is the acquisition, recording, organization, retrieval, display, and dissemination of information. In recent years, the term "information processing" has often been applied to computer-based operations specifically.

In popular usage, the term "information" refers to facts and opinions provided and received during the course of daily life: one obtains information directly from other living beings, from mass media, from electronic data banks, and from all sorts of observations of the surrounding environment. A person using such facts and opinions generates more information; some of this is communicated to others during speech, by instructions, in letters and documents, and through other media. Information organized according to some logical relationships is referred to as a body of knowledge. Application of knowledge (or skills) yields expertise, and additional insights may yield wisdom.

Use of the term "information" is not restricted exclusively to its communication via natural language. Information is also registered and communicated through art and by facial expressions and gestures or by such other physical responses as shivering. Moreover, every living entity is endowed with information in the form of the genetic code.

Altogether, these pieces of information permeate the physical and mental world, and their variety is such that it has defied so far all attempts at a unified definition of information.

Interest in information phenomena increased dramatically in the 20th century. In the second decade of the 21st century they are studied in a number of disciplines, including philosophy, physics, biology, linguistics, information and computer science, electronic and communications engineering, management science, and the social sciences. On the commercial side, the information service industry has become one of the newer industries worldwide. Almost all other industries—manufacturing and service—are increasingly concerned with information and its handling. The different, though often overlapping, viewpoints and phenomena of these fields lead to different (and sometimes conflicting) concepts and definitions of information.

Basic Concepts

Interest in how information is communicated and how its carriers convey meaning has long occupied a field of inquiry called semiotics—the study of signs and sign phenomena. Signs are the intricate elements of communication and the carriers of meaning. The American philosopher, mathematician, and physicist Charles S. Peirce is credited with having pointed out the three dimensions of signs: the body or medium of the sign, the object that the sign designates, and the interpretation of the sign. Another American philosopher, Charles W. Morris, designated these three sign dimensions syntactic, semantic, and pragmatic, the names by which they are known today. (The three terms stem from their use in linguistics. *Syntactic* refers to syntax, or the way in which words are put together to form phrases, clauses, or sentences. *Semantic* refers to the meanings of words and phrases. *Pragmatic* indicates a way of handling something in a reasonable and logical way.)

Information processes are executed by information processors. For a given information processor, whether physical or biological, a token is an object, devoid of meaning, that the processor recognizes as being totally different from other tokens. A group of such unique tokens recognized by a processor constitutes its basic "alphabet." For example, the dot, dash, and space constitute the basic token alphabet of a Morse-code processor. Objects that carry meaning are represented by patterns of tokens called symbols. The latter combine to form symbolic expressions that constitute inputs to or outputs from information processes and are stored in the processor memory.

Information processors are components of an information system. An abstract model of an information system features four basic elements: processor, memory, receptor, and effector. The processor has several functions: (1) to carry out elementary information processes on symbolic expressions, (2) to store temporarily in the processor's short-term

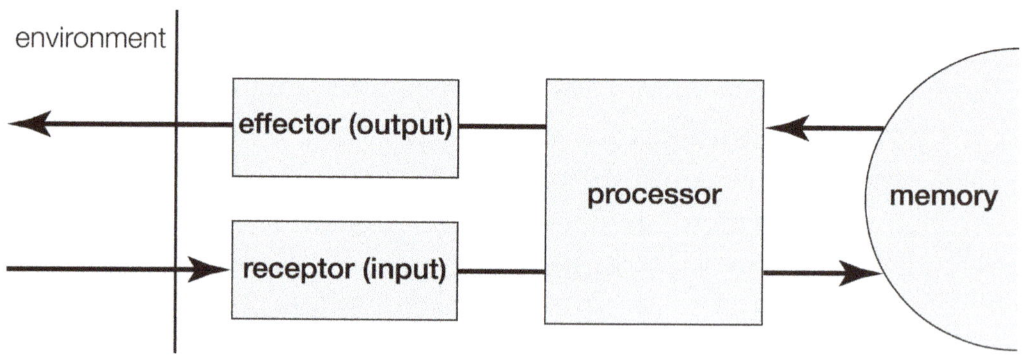

An illustration of the structure of an information system features the processor, memory, receptor, and effector.

memory the input and output expressions on which these processes operate and that they generate, (3) to schedule execution of these processes, and (4) to change this sequence of operations in accordance with the contents of the short-term memory. The memory stores symbolic expressions, including those that represent composite information processes, called programs. The two other components, the receptor and the effector, are input and output mechanisms whose functions are, respectively, to receive symbolic expressions or stimuli from the external environment for manipulation by the processor and to emit the processed structures back to the environment.

The power of this model is the ability of its component processors to carry out a small number of elementary information processes: reading; comparing; creating, modifying, and naming; copying; storing; and writing. The model has been found useful to help explain information systems based on sequential information processors—that is, processors of information presented in a series or sequence.

In nature, however, information processes are not strictly sequential. This has brought increased attention in recent decades to the study of the human brain as an information processor of the parallel type. The cognitive sciences—the interdisciplinary field that focuses on the study of the human mind—have contributed to the development of neurocomputers. These are a new class of parallel, distributed-information processors that mimic the functioning of the human brain, including its capabilities for self-organization and learning. These so-called neural networks are mathematical models inspired by the neural circuit network of the human brain. They are frequently applied in areas such as pattern recognition, control of industrial processes, and finance, as well as in many research disciplines.

INFORMATION AS A RESOURCE AND COMMODITY

In the late 20th century, information acquired two major useful connotations. On the one hand, information is considered an economic resource, somewhat on par with other resources such as labor, material, and capital. This view stems from evidence that the possession, manipulation, and use of information can increase the cost-effectiveness of many physical and cognitive processes. The rise in information-processing activities in industrial manufacturing as well as in human problem solving has been remarkable. Analysis of one of the three traditional divisions of the economy, the service sector, shows a sharp increase in information-intensive activities since the beginning of the 20th century. By 1975 these activities accounted for half of the labor force of the United States, giving rise to the so-called information society.

As an individual and societal resource, information has some interesting characteristics that separate it from the traditional notions of economic resources. Unlike other resources, information is expansive, with

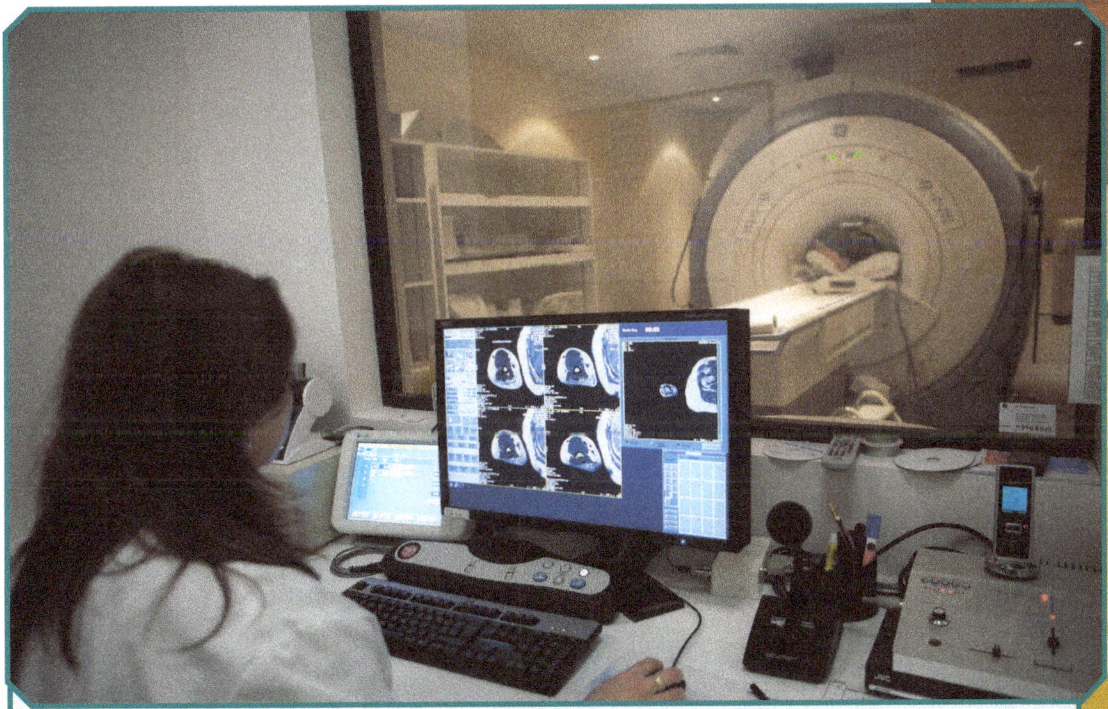

A technician uses a magnetic resonance imaging (MRI) scanner to create information—high-definition, three-dimensional pictures of a patient's arm tissues—for diagnostic purposes.

limits apparently imposed only by time and human cognitive capabilities. Its expansiveness is attributable to the following: (1) it is naturally diffusive, (2) it reproduces rather than being consumed through use, and (3) it can be shared only—that is, it is not exchanged in transactions. At the same time, information is compressible, both syntactically and semantically. Coupled with its ability to be substituted for other economic resources, its transportability at very high speeds, and its ability to impart advantages to the holder of information, these characteristics are at the base of such societal industries as research, education, publishing, marketing, and even politics. Societal concern with the oversight and care of information resources has extended from the traditional domain of libraries and archives to encompass organizational, institutional, and governmental information under the umbrella of information resource management.

The second perception of information is that it is an economic commodity, which helps to stimulate the worldwide growth of a new segment of national economies—the information service sector. Taking advantage of the properties of information and building on the perception of its individual and societal utility and value, this sector provides a broad range of information products and services. By 1992 the market share of the U.S. information service sector had grown to about $25 billion. This was equivalent to about one-seventh of the country's computer market, which, in turn, represented roughly 40 percent of the global market in computers in that year. However, the probable convergence of computers and television and its impact on information services, entertainment, and education are likely to restructure the respective market shares of the information industry. In 2011 spending in research and development alone in U.S. information and communications technologies reached $126.3 billion.

CHAPTER 3

ELEMENTS OF INFORMATION PROCESSING

Humans receive information with their senses: sounds through hearing; images and text through sight; shape, temperature, and affection through touch; and odors through smell. To interpret the signals received from the senses, humans have developed and learned complex systems of languages consisting of alphabets of symbols and stimuli and the associated rules of usage. This has enabled humans to recognize the objects they see, understand the messages they read or hear, and comprehend the signs received through the tactile and olfactory senses.

The carriers of information-conveying signs received by the senses are energy phenomena—audio waves, light waves, and chemical and electrochemical stimuli. In engineering parlance, humans are receptors of analog signals; and, by a somewhat loose convention, the messages conveyed via these carriers are called analog-form information, or simply analog information. Until the development of the digital computer, cognitive information was stored and processed only in analog form, basically through the technologies of printing, photography, and telephony.

Although humans are adept at processing information stored in their memories, analog information stored external to the mind is not processed easily. Modern information technology greatly facilitates the manipulation of externally stored information as a result of its representation as digital signals—i.e., as the presence or absence of energy (electricity, light, or magnetism). Information represented digitally in two-state, or binary, form is often referred to as digital information. Modern information systems are characterized by extensive metamorphoses of analog and digital information. With respect to information storage and communication, the transition from analog to digital information is so pervasive as to bring a historic transformation of the manner in which humans create, access, and use information.

Acquiring Analog Information

The principal categories of information sources useful in modern information systems are text, video, and voice. One of the first ways in which prehistoric humans communicated was by sound—sounds represented concepts such as pleasure, anger, and fear, as well as objects of the surrounding environment, including food and tools. Sounds assumed their meaning by convention—namely, by the use to which they were consistently put. Combining parts of sound allowed representation of more complex concepts and gradually led to the development of speech and eventually to spoken languages.

For information to be communicated broadly, it needs to be stored external to human memory; because accumulation of human experience, knowledge, and learning would be severely limited without such storage, the development of writing systems was made necessary.

Civilization can be traced to the time when humans began to associate abstract shapes with concepts and with the sounds of speech that represented them. Early recorded representations were those of visually perceived objects and events, as, for example, the animals and activities depicted in Paleolithic cave drawings. The evolution of writing systems proceeded through the early development of pictographic languages, in which a symbol would represent an entire concept. Such symbols would go through many changes of shape in which the resemblance between each symbol and the object it stood for gradually disappeared, but its semantic meaning would become more precise. As the conceptual world of humans became larger, the symbols—called ideographs—grew in number. Modern Chinese, a present-day result of this evolutionary direction of a pictographic writing system, has upwards of 50,000 ideographs.

At some point in the evolution of written languages, the method of representation shifted from the pictographic to the phonetic: speech sounds began to be represented by an alphabet of graphic symbols. Combinations of a relatively small set of such symbols could stand for more complex concepts as words, phrases, and sentences. The invention of the written phonetic alphabet is thought to have taken place during the 2nd millennium BCE. The pragmatic advantages of alphabetic writing systems over the pictographic became apparent twice in the past millennium: after the invention of the movable-type printing press in the 15th century and again with the development of information processing by electronic means since the mid-1940s.

From the time early humans learned to represent concepts symbolically, they used whatever materials were readily available in nature for recording. The Sumerian cuneiform, a wedge-shaped writing system, was impressed by a stylus into soft clay tablets, which were subsequently hardened by drying in the sun or the oven. The earliest Chinese writing, dating to the 2nd millennium BCE, is preserved on animal bone and shell, while early writing in India was done on palm leaves and birch bark. Applications of technology yielded other materials for writing. The Chinese had recorded their pictographs on silk, using brushes made from animal hair, long before they invented paper. The Egyptians first wrote on cotton, but they began using papyrus sheets and rolls made from the fibrous lining of the papyrus plant during the 4th millennium BCE. The reed brush and a palette of ink were the implements with which they wrote hieroglyphic script. Writing on parchment, a material that was superior to papyrus and was made from the prepared skins of animals, became commonplace about 200 BCE, some 300 years after its first recorded use, and the quill pen replaced the reed brush. By the 4th century CE, parchment came to be the principal writing material in Europe.

Paper was invented in China at the beginning of the 2nd century CE, and for some 600 years its use was confined to East Asia. In 751 CE Arab and Chinese armies clashed at the Battle of Talas, near Samarkand; among the Chinese taken captive were some papermakers from whom the Arabs learned the techniques. From the 7th century on, paper became the dominant writing material of the Islamic world. Papermaking finally reached Spain and Sicily in the 12th century, and it took another three centuries before it was practiced in Germany.

With the invention of printing from movable type, typesetting became the standard method of creating copy. Typesetting was done manually until the adoption of a typewriter-like keyboard in the 19th century. In fact, it was the typewriter that mechanized the process of recording original text. Although the typewriter was invented during the early 18th century in England, the first practical version, constructed by the American inventor Christopher Latham

Lillian Sholes, the daughter of inventor Christopher Latham Sholes, types on one of her father's machines in 1872.

Sholes, did not appear until 1867. The mechanical typewriter finally found wide use after World War I. Today its electronic variant, the computer, is used pervasively to record original text.

Recording of original nontextual (image) information was a manual process until the development of photography during the early decades of the 19th century; drawing and carving were the principal early means of recording graphics. Other techniques were developed alongside printing—for example, etching in stone and metal. The invention of film and the photographic process added a new dimension to information acquisition: for the first time, complex visual images of the real world could be captured accurately. Photography provided a method of storing information in less space and more accurately than was previously possible with narrative information.

During the 20th century, versatile electromagnetic media opened up new possibilities for capturing original analog information. Magnetic audiotape is used to capture speech and music, and magnetic videotape provides a low-cost medium for recording analog voice and video signals directly and simultaneously. Magnetic technology has other uses in the direct recording of analog information, including alphanumerics. Magnetic characters, bar codes, and special marks are printed on checks, labels, and forms for subsequent sensing by magnetic or optical readers and conversion to digital form. Banks, educational institutions, and the retail industry rely heavily on this technology. Nonetheless, paper and film continue to be the dominant media for direct storage of textual and visual information in analog form.

Acquiring Digital Information

The versatility of modern information systems stems from their ability to represent information electronically as digital signals, and to manipulate it automatically at exceedingly high speeds. Information is stored in binary devices, the basic components of digital technology. Because these devices exist only in one of two states, information is represented in them either as the absence or the presence of energy (electric pulse). The two states of binary devices are conveniently designated by the binary digits, or bits, zero (0) and one (1).

In this manner, alphabetic symbols of natural-language writing systems can be represented digitally as combinations of zeros (no pulse) and ones (pulse). Tables of equivalences of alphanumeric characters and strings of binary digits are called coding systems—in digital technology, these are the counterpart of writing systems. A combination of three binary digits can represent up to eight such characters; one comprising four digits, up to 16 characters; and so on. The choice of a coding system depends on the size of the character set to be represented. The widely used systems are the American Standard Code for Information Interchange (ASCII), a seven- or eight-bit code representing the English alphabet, numerals, and certain special characters of the standard computer keyboard; and the corresponding eight-bit Extended Binary Coded Decimal Interchange Code (EBCDIC), used for computers produced by IBM (International Business Machines Corp.) and most compatible systems. Digital representation of a character by eight bits is called a byte.

The seven-bit ASCII code is capable of representing up to 128 alphanumeric and special characters. This is sufficient to accommodate the writing systems of many phonetic scripts, including Latin and Cyrillic. Some alphabetic scripts require more than seven bits; for example, the Arabic alphabet, also used in the Urdu and Persian languages, has

ASCII Code - Character to Binary

Character	Binary
0	0011 0000
1	0011 0001
2	0011 0010
3	0011 0011
4	0011 0100
5	0011 0101
6	0011 0110
7	0011 0110
8	0011 1000
9	0011 1001
A	0100 0001
B	0100 0010
C	0100 0011
D	0100 0100
E	0100 0101
F	0100 0110
G	0100 0111
H	0100 1000
I	0100 1001
J	0100 1010
K	0100 1011
L	0100 1100
M	0100 1101
N	0100 1110
O	0100 1111
P	0101 0000
Q	0101 0001
R	0101 0010
S	0101 0011
T	0101 0100
U	0101 0101
V	0101 0110
W	0101 0111
X	0101 1000
Y	0101 1001
Z	0101 1010
a	0110 0001
b	0110 0010
c	0110 0011
d	0110 0100
e	0110 0101
f	0110 0110
g	0110 0110
h	0110 1000
i	0110 1001
j	0110 1010
k	0110 1011
l	0110 1100
m	0110 1101
n	0110 1110
o	0110 1111
p	0111 0000
q	0111 0001
r	0111 0010
s	0111 0011
t	0111 0100
u	0111 0101
v	0111 0110
w	0111 0111
x	0111 1000
y	0111 1001
z	0111 1010
:	0011 1010
;	0011 1011
?	0011 1111
.	0010 1110
'	0010 1111
!	0010 0001
,	0010 1100
"	0010 0010
(	0010 1000
)	0010 1001
space	0010 0000

American Standard Code for Information Interchange (ASCII) is a code representing letters, numerals, and other symbols of a computer keyboard for information processing. This example shows an eight-bit code.

28 consonantal characters (as well as several vowels and diacritical marks), but each of these may have four shapes, depending on its position in the word.

For digital representation of nonalphabetic writing systems, even the eight-bit code accommodating 256 characters is inadequate. Some writing systems that use Chinese characters, for example, have more than 50,000 ideographs (the minimal standard font for the Hanzi system in Chinese and the kanji system in Japanese has about 7,000 ideographs). Digital representation of such scripts can be accomplished in three ways. One approach is to develop a phonetic character set; the Chinese Pinyin, the Korean Hangul, and the Japanese hiragana phonetic schemes all have alphabetic sets similar in number to the Latin alphabet. Because the use of phonetic alphabets in Asian cultures is not yet widespread, they may be converted to ideographic by means of a dictionary lookup. A second technique is to decompose ideographs into a small number of elementary signs called strokes, the sum of which constitutes a shape-oriented, nonphonetic alphabet. The third approach is to use more than eight bits to encode the large numbers of ideographs; for instance, two bytes can represent uniquely more than 65,000 ideographs. Because the eight-bit ASCII code is inadequate for a number of writing systems, either because they are nonalphabetic or because their phonetic scripts possess large numbers of diacritical marks, the computer industry in 1991 began formulating a new international coding standard based on 16 bits.

Recording Media

Punched cards and perforated paper tape were once widely used to store data in binary form. Today they have been supplanted by media based on electromagnetic and electro-optic technologies except in a few special applications.

Present-day storage media are of two types: random- and serial (sequential)-access. In random-access media, the time required for accessing a given piece of data is independent of its location. In serial-access media, access time depends on data location and the position of the read-write head. The typical serial-access medium is magnetic tape. The storage density of magnetic tape has increased over the years, mainly by increases in the number of tracks packed across the width of the tape.

While magnetic tape remains a popular choice in applications requiring low-cost auxiliary storage and data exchange, new tape variants began entering the market of the 1990s. Video recording tape was adapted for digital storage. Digital audiotape (DAT) surpassed all tape storage devices in offering the highest areal data densities. DAT technology used a helical-scan recording method in which both the tape and the recording head move simultaneously, which allows very high recording densities. Early four-millimeter DAT cassettes had a capacity of up to eight billion bytes (eight gigabytes).

Another type of magnetic storage medium, the magnetic disk, provides rapid, random access to data. This device, developed in 1962, consists of either an aluminum or a plastic platen coated with a metallic material. Information is recorded on a disk by turning the charge of the read-write head on and off, which produces magnetic "dots" representing binary digits in circular tracks. A block of data on a given track can be accessed without having to pass over a large portion of its contents sequentially, as in the case of tape. Data-retrieval time is reduced dramatically. Hard disk drives built into personal computers today may have storage capacities of up to several hundred gigabytes. Large computers using disk cartridges can provide virtually unlimited mass storage.

During the 1970s the floppy disk—a small, flexible disk—was introduced for use in personal computers and other microcomputer systems. Compared with the storage capacity of the conventional hard disk, that of the "soft" diskette was low—under three million characters. This medium was used primarily for loading and backing up personal computers.

An entirely different kind of recording and storage medium, the optical disc, became available during the early 1980s. The optical disc makes use of laser technology: digital data are

Floppy disks, beginning in the 1970s, and compact disks (CDs), beginning in the 1980s, were used to store and back up data on personal computers.

recorded by burning a series of microscopic holes, or pits, with a laser beam into thin metallic film on the surface of a 4-¾ inch (12-centimeter) plastic disc. In this way, information from magnetic tape is encoded on a master disc; subsequently, the master is replicated by a process called stamping. In the read mode, low-intensity laser light is reflected off the disc surface and is "read" by light-sensitive diodes. The radiant energy received by the diodes varies according to the presence of the pits, and this input is digitized by the diode circuits. The digital signals are then converted to analog information on a video screen or in printout form.

With the introduction of this technology, three main types of optical storage media became available: (1) rewritable, (2) write-once read-many (WORM), and (3) compact disc read-only memory (CD-ROM). Rewritable discs are functionally equivalent to magnetic disks, although the former are slower. WORM discs are used as an archival storage medium to enter data once and retrieve it many times. CD-ROMs are the preferred medium for electronic distribution of digital libraries and software. To raise storage capacity, optical discs are arranged into "jukeboxes" holding as many as 10 million pages of text or more than one terabyte (one trillion bytes) of image data. The high storage capacities and random access of the magneto-optical, rewritable discs are particularly suited for storing multimedia information, in which text, image, and sound are combined.

RECORDING TECHNIQUES

Digitally stored information is commonly referred to as data, and its analog counterpart is called source data. Vast quantities of nondocument analog data are collected, digitized, and compressed automatically by means of appropriate instruments in fields such as astronomy, environmental monitoring, scientific experimentation and modeling, and national security. The capture of information generated by humankind, in the form of packages of symbols called documents, is accomplished by manual and, increasingly, automatic techniques. Data are entered manually by striking the keys of a keyboard, touching a computer screen, or writing by hand on a digital tablet or its variant, the so-called pen computer. Manual data entry, a slow and error-prone process, is facilitated to a degree by special computer programs that include editing software, which are used to insert formatting commands, verify spelling, and make text changes, and document-formatting software, used to arrange and rearrange text and graphics flexibly on the output page.

It is estimated that five percent of all documents in the United States exist in digitized form and that two-thirds of the paper documents cannot be digitized by keyboard transcription because they contain drawings

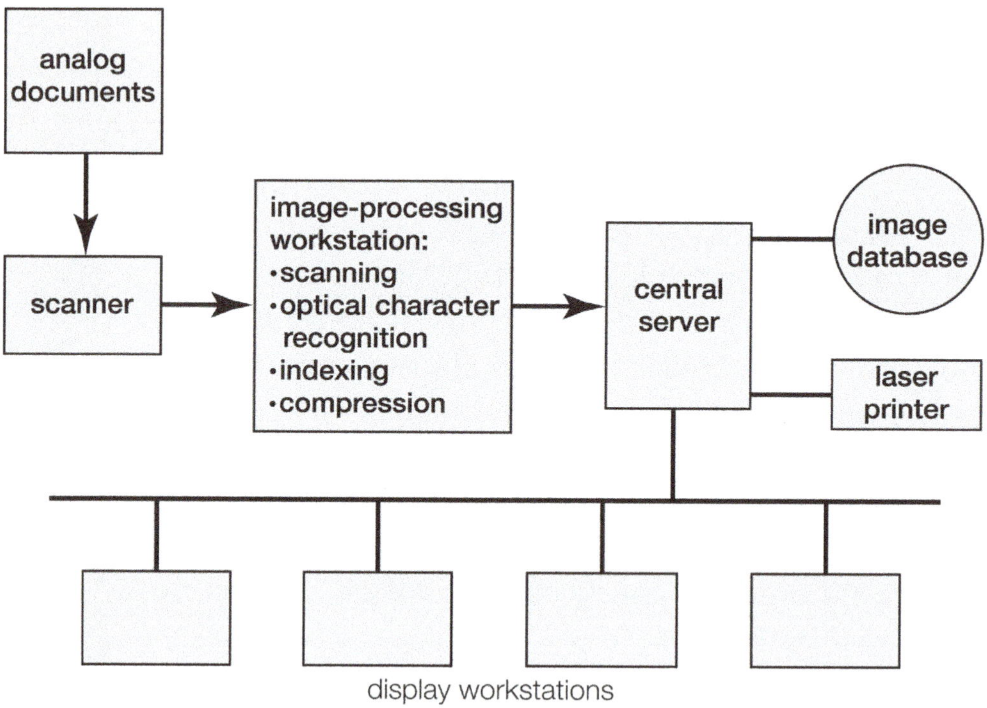

In document imaging, a scanner creates a document's digital representation and an image scanner generates pixels and binary digits. The bits are compressed by a controller, stored, and then processed and retrieved by a server.

or still images and because such transcription would be highly uneconomical. Such documents are digitized economically by a process called document imaging. This process is diagrammed on the previous page.

Document imaging uses digital scanners to generate a digital representation of a document page. An image scanner divides the page into minute picture areas called pixels and produces an array of binary digits, each representing the brightness of a pixel. The resulting stream of bits is enhanced and compressed (to as little as 10 percent of the original volume) by a device called an image controller and is stored on a magnetic or optical medium. A large storage capacity is required, because it takes about 45,000 bytes to store a typical compressed text page of 2,500 characters and as much as 1,000,000 bytes to store a page containing an image. Aside from document imaging applications, digital scanning is used for transmission of documents via facsimile, in satellite photography, and in other applications.

An image scanner digitizes an entire document page for storage and display as an image and does not recognize characters and words of text. The stored material therefore cannot be linguistically manipulated by text processing and other software techniques. When such manipulation is desired, a software program performs the optical character recognition (OCR) function. OCR converts each optically scanned character into an electric signal and compares it with a internally stored representation of an alphabet of characters. The function can then select a character from its stored "library" of characters that matches the scanned character most closely. Sophisticated modern-day OCR programs can distinguish shapes, sizes, and pitch of symbols, including handwriting—and learn from experience.

Still photographs can be digitized by scanning or transferred from film to a digital disc holding more than 100 images. A relatively recent development, the digital camera, makes it possible to bypass the film/paper step completely by capturing the image into the camera's memory or a special diskette and then transferring it to a personal computer. Both technologies produce a graphics file, so the image can be edited using suitable software.

The digital recording of sound is important because speech is the most frequently used natural carrier of communicable information. Direct capture of sound into personal computers is accomplished by means of a digital signal processor (DSP) chip, a special-purpose device built into the computer to perform array-processing operations. The conversion of analog audio signals to digital recordings is a commonplace process that has been used for years by the telecommunications and entertainment industries. Automatic speech recognition—analogous to the recognition of characters and words in text by means of optical character recognition—allows digital transcription of spoken language into readable text in real time. This technology has wide applications, from medical documentation to education, and provides a great benefit to individuals with certain disabilities.

By the beginning of the 1990s, the technology to record (or convert), store in digital form, and edit all visually and aurally perceived signals—text, graphics, still images, animation, motion video, and sound—had become available and affordable. These capabilities opened a way for a new kind of multimedia document that employs print, video, and sound to generate more powerful and colorful messages, communicate them securely at electronic speeds, and allow them to be modified almost at will. The traditional business letter, newspaper, journal, and book will no longer be the same.

INVENTORY OF RECORDED INFORMATION

The development of recording media and techniques enabled society to begin building a store of human knowledge. The idea of collecting and organizing written records is thought to have originated in Sumer about 5,000 years ago; Egyptian writing was introduced soon after. Early collections of Sumerian and Egyptian writings, recorded in cuneiform on clay tablets and in hieroglyphic script on papyrus, contained information about legal and economic transactions. In these and other early document collections (e.g., those of China produced during the Shang dynasty in the 2nd millennium BCE and Buddhist collections in India dating to the 5th century BCE), it is difficult to separate the concepts of the archive and the library.

From the Middle East the concept of document collections penetrated the Greco-Roman world. Roman kings institutionalized the population and property census as early as the 6th century BCE. The great Library of Alexandria, established in the 3rd century BCE, is best known as a large collection of papyri containing inventories of

Halle in der Alexandrinischen Bibliothek.

The Library of Alexandria in Egypt was the most famous library of Classical antiquity. In many ways the Library of Alexandria was an early administrative information system because it enabled the maintenance, storage, and retrieval of documents.

property, taxes, and other payments by citizens to their rulers and to each other. It is, in short, the ancient equivalent of today's administrative information systems.

The scholarly splendor of the Islamic world from the 8th to the 13th century CE can in large part be attributed to the maintenance of public and private book libraries. The Bayt al-Ḥikmah ("House of Wisdom"), founded in 830 in Baghdad, contained a public library with a large collection of materials on a wide range of subjects. The 10th-century library of Caliph al-Ḥakam in Cordova, Spain, boasted more than 400,000 books.

PRIMARY AND SECONDARY LITERATURE

The late but rapid development of European libraries from the 16th century on followed the invention of printing from movable type, which spurred the growth of the printing and publishing industries. Since the early 17th century, literature has become the principal medium for disseminating knowledge. The phrase primary literature is used to designate original information in various printed formats: newspapers, monographs, conference proceedings, scholarly and trade journals, reports, patents, bulletins, and newsletters. The scholarly journal, the classic medium of scientific communication, first appeared in 1665. Three hundred years later the number of periodical titles published in the world was estimated at more than 60,000.

The sheer quantity of printed information has for some time prevented any individual from fully absorbing even a minuscule fraction of it. Such devices as tables of contents, summaries, and indexes of various types, which aid in identifying and locating relevant information in primary literature, have been in use since the 16th century and led to the development of what is termed secondary literature during the 19th century.

The purpose of secondary literature is to "filter" the primary information sources, usually by subject area, and provide the indicators to this literature in the form of reviews, abstracts, and indexes. Over the past 100 years there has evolved a system of abstracting and indexing services that acts as a gateway to authors, subjects, publishers, dates (and languages) of publication, and citations. The professional activity associated with these access-facilitating tools is called documentation.

The quantity of printed materials makes it impossible, as well as undesirable, for any institution to acquire and house more than a small portion of it. The husbanding of recorded information has become a matter of public policy, as many countries have established national libraries and archives to direct the orderly acquisition of analog-form documents and records. These institutions alone are not able to keep up with the output of such documents and records; thus new forms of cooperative planning and sharing recorded materials are evolving—namely, public and private, national and regional library networks and consortia.

DATABASES

The emergence of digital technology in the mid-20th century and its rapid increase in the 21st century has affected humankind's inventory of recorded information dramatically. During the early 1960s computers were used to digitize text for the first time; the purpose was to reduce the cost and time required to publish two American abstracting journals, the *Index Medicus* of the National Library of Medicine and the *Scientific and Technical Aerospace Reports* of the National Aeronautics and Space Administration (NASA). By the late 1960s such bodies of digitized alphanumeric information, known as bibliographic and numeric databases, constituted a new type of information resource. This resource is husbanded outside the traditional repositories of information (libraries and archives) by database "vendors." Advances in computer storage, telecommunications, software for computer sharing, and automated techniques of text indexing and searching fueled the development of an online database service industry. Meanwhile, electronic applications to bibliographic control in libraries and archives have led to the development of computerized catalogs and of union

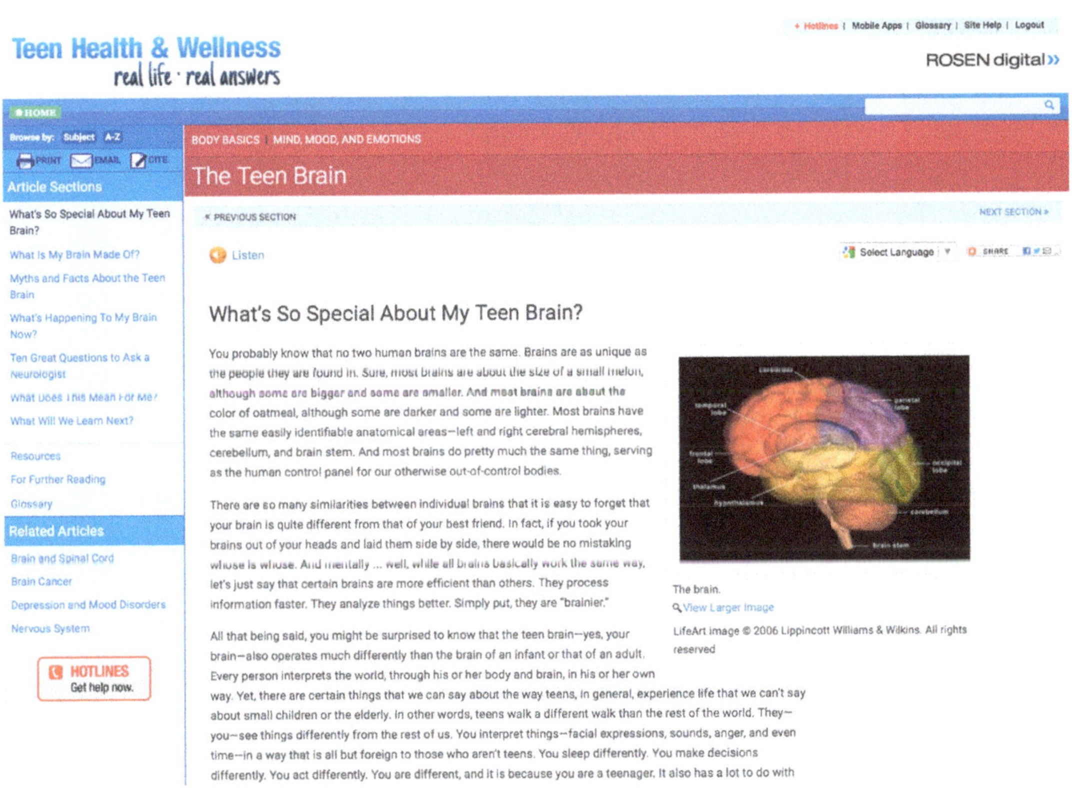

Online databases make information accessible to people in their homes, offices, libraries, and even on smartphones with the use of certain mobile applications (apps).

HOW DATABASES WORK

A database is a collection of data that is specially organized for rapid search by computer. The data are interrelated so that a user can easily call up all the information that meets specific criteria. Users can add, change, delete, and retrieve information in a database through various data-processing operations.

Some databases store the texts of documents, while others store mainly numbers such as statistics, financial data, and raw scientific and technical data. Small databases can be maintained on personal-computer systems for use by individuals at home. These and larger databases have become increasingly important in business life, in part because they are now commonly designed to be integrated with other office software, including spreadsheet programs.

Databases are frequently used in e-commerce. Other typical examples of commercial databases include employee records, airline reservations, and hospital medical records. The largest databases are usually maintained by governmental agencies, business organizations, and universities.

A database is stored as a file or a set of files. The information in the files may be broken down into records, each of which contains one or more fields. Fields are the basic units of data storage. A field may contain, for example, an employee's last name, the name of a library book, the text of a journal article, a customer's credit card number, or the quantity of grapes in stock at a grocery store. The data in the fields are cross-referenced, or linked, so users can rapidly search, rearrange, group, and select fields in many records to retrieve or create reports on particular collections of data.

Databases can be structured in various ways, but relational databases are the most common. In this type of

database, the fields are organized into a series of linked tables consisting of rows and columns. Payroll data, for example, can be stored in one table and personnel benefits data in another; complete information on an employee can be obtained by joining the tables on employee identification number.

Users retrieve information from a database by formulating queries. Typically, one types words or numbers into a search box, and the computer searches the database for a corresponding sequence of characters. A user can request, for example, all records in which the contents of the field for a person's last name is the word Smith.

catalogs in library networks. These also have helped introduce comprehensive automation programs in these institutions.

The explosive growth of communications networks toward the end of the 20th century accelerated establishment of the "virtual library." At the leading edge of this development was public-domain information. Residing in thousands of databases distributed worldwide, a growing portion of this vast resource is now accessible almost instantaneously via the Internet and nonacademic organizations. Internet resources of electronic information include selected library catalogs, collected works of the literature, some abstracting journals, full-text electronic journals, encyclopedias, scientific data from numerous disciplines, software archives, demographic registers, daily news summaries, environmental reports, and prices in commodity markets, as well as hundreds of thousands of e-mail and social-network messages. To be useful, however, this vast inventory of information must be systematically organized and retrievable in items relevant to human needs.

ORGANIZATION AND RETRIEVAL OF INFORMATION

In any collection, physical objects are related by order. The ordering may be random or according to some characteristic called a key. Such characteristics may be properties of the objects (e.g., size, shape, or color), or they may be assigned from an agreed-upon set, such as date of purchase. The values of the key are arranged in a sorting sequence that depends on the type of key: alphanumeric key values may be sorted in alphabetic sequence, while other types may be sorted on the basis of similarity in class, such as books on a particular subject.

In most cases, order is imposed on a set of information objects for two reasons: to create their inventory and to facilitate locating specific objects in the set. There also exist other, secondary objectives for selecting a particular ordering—for example, conservation of space or economy of effort in fetching objects. Unless the objects in a collection are replicated, any ordering scheme is one-dimensional and unable to meet all the functions of ordering with equal effectiveness. The main approach for overcoming some of the limitations of one-dimensional ordering of recorded information relies on extended description of its content and, for analog-form information, of some features of the physical items. This approach employs various tools of content analysis that subsequently facilitate accessing and searching recorded information.

DESCRIPTION AND ANALYSIS OF ANALOG RECORDS

The collections of libraries and archives, the primary repositories of analog-form information, constitute one-dimensional ordering of physical materials in print (documents), in image form (maps and photographs), or in audio-video format (recordings and videotapes). To break away from the confines of one-dimensional ordering, librarianship has developed an extensive set of attributes for use in describing each item in the collection. These attributes are assigned using cataloging rules. Descriptive cataloging is the extraction of bibliographic elements (author names, title, publisher, date of publication, etc.) from each item; the assignment of subject categories or headings to such items is termed subject cataloging.

Conceptually, the library catalog is a table or matrix in which each row describes a discrete physical item and each column provides values of the assigned key. When such a catalog is represented digitally in a computer, any attribute can serve as the ordering key. By sorting the catalog on different keys, it is possible to produce a variety of indexes as well as subject bibliographies. More important, any of the attributes of a computerized catalog becomes a search key (access point) to the collection, surpassing the utility of the traditional card catalog.

The most useful access key to analog-form items is subject. The extensive lists of subject headings of library classification schemes provide a gross access tool to the content of the items. A technique called indexing provides a refinement over library subject headings. It consists of extracting from the item or assigning to it subject and other "descriptors"—words or phrases denoting significant concepts (such as topics or names) that occur in or characterize the content of the record. Indexing frequently accompanies abstracting, a technique for condensing the full text of a document into a short summary that contains its principal ideas. Computer-printed, indexed abstracting journals keep users informed of primary information sources.

Description and Analysis of Digital Records

The description of an electronic document generally follows the principles of bibliographic cataloging if the document is part of a database that is expected to be accessed directly and individually. When the database is part of a universe of globally distributed database servers that are searchable in parallel, the matter of document naming is more challenging. The document description must include the name of the database server—i.e., its physical location. Because database servers may delete particular documents, the description must also contain a pointer to the document's logical address (the generating organization). In the cataloging of digital documents, physical attributes such as format and size are unimportant in a universal document-naming scheme. On the other hand, the data type of the document (text, sound, etc.) is critical to its transmission and use.

Machine Indexing

The subject analysis of electronic text is accomplished by means of machine indexing, using one of two approaches: the assignment of subject descriptors from an unlimited vocabulary (free indexing) or their assignment from a list of authorized descriptors (controlled indexing). A collection of authorized descriptors is called an authority list or, if it also displays various relationships among descriptors such as hierarchy or synonymy, a thesaurus. The result of the indexing process is a computer file known as an inverted index, which is an alphabetic listing of descriptors and the addresses of their occurrence in the document body.

Full-text indexing, the use of every character string (word of a natural language) in the text as an index term, is an extreme case of free-text indexing: each word in the document (except function words such as articles and prepositions) becomes an access point to it. Used earlier to generate concordances in literary analysis and other computer applications in the humanities, full-text indexing placed great demands on computer storage because the resulting index is at least as large as the body of the text. Today, automatic full-text indexing capabilities are widely found in information-management software.

Text indexing may be supplemented by other syntactic techniques in order to increase its robustness. One such method is Standard Generalized Markup Language (SGML). This technique incorporates standard text markers used by editors to pinpoint document elements such as paragraphs and tables. In indexing spatial data such as maps and astronomical images, the textual index specifies search areas, each of which is further described by a set of coordi nates defining a rectangle or irregular polygon. These digital spatial document attributes are then used to retrieve and display a specific point or a selected region of the document.

Semantic Content Analysis

The analysis of digitally recorded natural-language information from the semantic viewpoint is a matter of considerable complexity, and it lies at the foundation of such applications as automatic question answering from a database or retrieval by unrestricted natural-language queries. The general approach has been that of computational linguistics: to derive representations of the syntactic and semantic relations between the linguistic elements of sentences and larger parts of the document.

Syntactic relations are described by parsing (decomposing) the grammar of sentences, as shown in the parsing graph below. In a semantic network, conceptual entities such

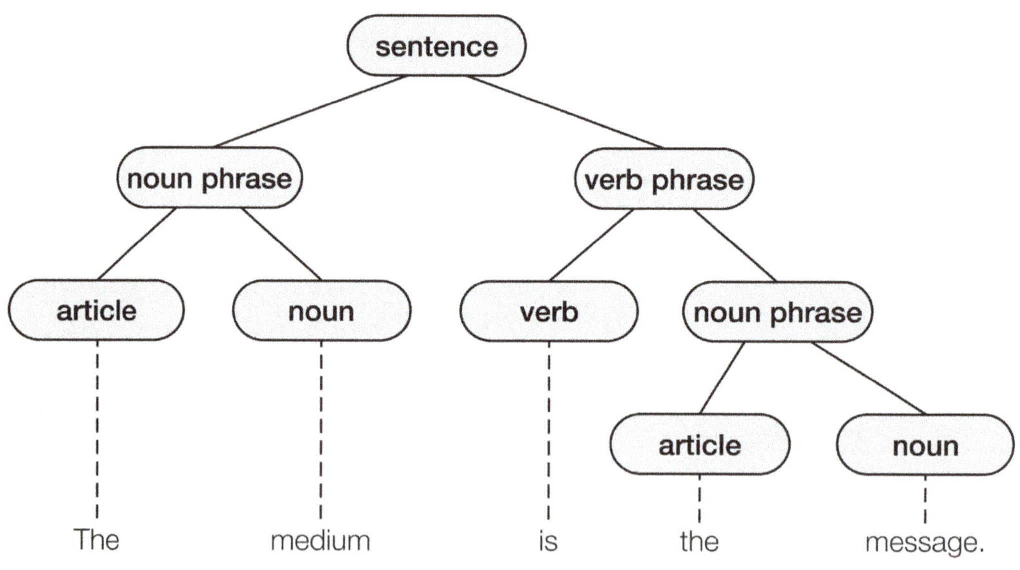

A parsing graph displays the parsing of the grammar in a sentence, where the sentence is divided into grammatical parts and each word's function is identified.

as objects, actions, or events are represented as a graph of linked nodes; this is illustrated in the graph on page 67.

Image Analysis

The content analysis of images is accomplished by two primary methods: image processing and pattern recognition. Image processing is a set of computational techniques for analyzing, enhancing, compressing, and reconstructing images. Pattern recognition is an information-reduction process: the assignment of visual or

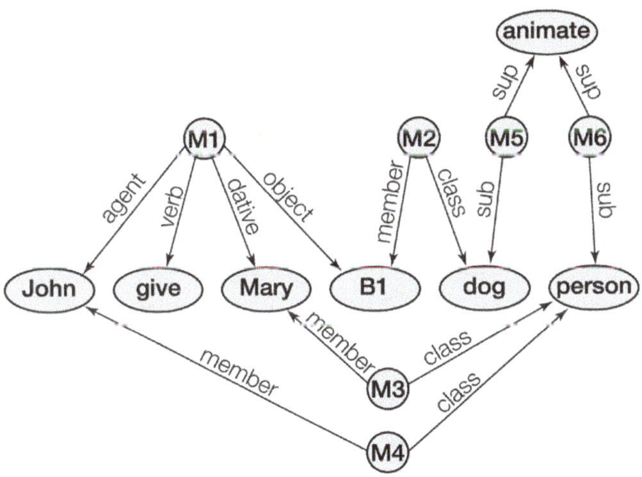

Nodes representing assertions and corresponding sentences are:
M1: John gives Mary a dog.
M2: What John gives to Mary is a dog.
M3: Mary is a person.
M4: John is a person.
M5: Dogs are animate beings.
M6: People are animate beings.

A semantic network is represented in this graph, where concepts (nodes) such as objects, actions, and events are linked (showing their relationships).

logical patterns to classes based on the features of these patterns and their relationships. Both image processing and pattern recognition have extensive applications in various areas, including astronomy, medicine, industrial robotics, and remote sensing by satellites.

SPEECH ANALYSIS

The immediate objective of content analysis of digital speech is the conversion of discrete sound elements into their alphanumeric equivalents. Once so represented, speech can be subjected to the same techniques of content analysis as natural-language text—that is, indexing and linguistic analysis. Converting speech elements into their alphanumeric counterparts is an intriguing problem because the "shape" of speech sounds embodies a wide range of many acoustic characteristics and because the linguistic elements of speech are not clearly distinguishable from one another.

Speech processing is complex and expensive in terms of storage capacity and computational requirements. State-of-the-art speech recognition systems can identify limited vocabularies and parts of distinctly spoken speech, and can be programmed to recognize tonal idiosyncrasies of individual speakers.

Storage Structures for Digital-form Information

Digital information is stored in complex patterns that make it feasible to address and operate on even the smallest element of symbolic expression, as well as on larger strings such as words or sentences and on images and sound.

From the viewpoint of digital information storage, it is useful to distinguish between structured data, such as inventories of objects that can be represented by short symbol strings and numbers, and unstructured data, such as the natural-language text of documents or pictorial images. The principal objective of all storage structures is to aid the processing of data elements on the basis of their relationships. The structures thus vary with the type of relationship they represent.

In information systems whose store consists of unstructured databases of natural-language records, the objective is to retrieve records (or portions thereof) based on the words or short phrases that constitute the query. An index that exists as a separate file provides information about the locations of words and phrases in the database records. This allows the relationships of interest (e.g., word adjacency) to be calculated from the index. Consequently, the database text itself can be stored as a simple ordered sequential file of records. The majority of the computations use the index, and they access the text file only to pull out the records or those portions that satisfy the result of the computations. The sequential file structure remains popular, with document-retrieval software intended for use with personal computers and CD-ROM databases.

When relationships between data elements must be represented as part of the records, two types of "chained" structures are commonly used: hierarchical and network. In the hierarchical file structure, records are arranged in a scheme resembling a family tree, with records related to one another from top to bottom. In the network file structure, records are arranged in groupings known as sets; these can be connected in any number of ways, giving rise to considerable flexibility. In both hierarchical and network structures, the relationships are shown by means of "pointers" (i.e., identifiers such as addresses or keys) that become part of the records.

Another type of database storage structure, the relational structure, has become increasingly popular since the late 1970s. Its major advantage over the hierarchical and network structures is the ability to handle unanticipated data relationships without pointers. The relational model was initially used for databases containing highly structured information. In the late 20th century it largely replaced the hierarchical and network models, and became the model of choice for large-scale information-management applications, both textual and multimedia.

Query Languages

The uses of databases are manifold. They provide a means of retrieving records or parts of records and performing various calculations before displaying the results. The interface by which such manipulations are specified is called the query language.

Early query languages were so complex that interacting with electronic databases could be done only by specially trained individuals. However, recent interfaces are more user-friendly, allowing casual users to access database information.

The main types of popular query modes are the menu, the "fill-in-the-blank" technique, and the structured query. The menu is especially suited for novices—it simply requires a user to choose from several alternatives displayed on the video terminal screen. The fill-in-the-blank technique is one in which the user is prompted to enter key words as search statements.

The structured query approach is effective with relational databases. It has a formal, powerful syntax that is in fact a programming language, and it is able to accommodate logical operators. One implementation of this approach is the Structured Query Language (SQL).

Structured query languages support database searching and other operations by using commands such as "find," "delete," "print," "sum," and so forth. The sentence-like structure of an SQL query resembles natural language except that its syntax is limited and fixed. Instead of using an SQL statement, it is possible to represent queries in tabular form. The technique, referred to as query-by-example (or QBE), displays an empty tabular form and expects the searcher to enter the search specifications into appropriate columns. The program then constructs an SQL-type query from the table and executes it.

The most flexible query language is of course natural language. The use of natural-language sentences in a constrained form to search databases is allowed by some commercial database management software.

Information Searching and Retrieval

State-of-the-art approaches to retrieving information employ two generic techniques: (1) matching words in the query against the database index (key-word searching) and (2) traversing the database with the aid of hypertext or hypermedia links.

Key-word searches can be made either more general or narrower in scope by means of logical operators (e.g., terms such as "or" or "and"). Because of the semantic ambiguities involved in free-text indexing, the precision of the key-word retrieval technique is far from ideal, and various modifications have been introduced to improve it. In one such enhancement, the search output is sorted by degree of relevance, based on a statistical match between the key words in the query and in the document. Key-word searching has been the dominant approach to text retrieval since the early 1960s.

The exponential growth of the use of computer networks in the 1990s forewarned of significant changes in systems and techniques of information retrieval. The wide-area information service is a good example. A number of these systems began operating in the early 1990s on the Internet. In these systems, a user's personal computer or terminal (called a client) could search simultaneously a number of databases maintained on heterogeneous computers, known as servers. These servers were located at different geographic sites, and their databases contained different data types and often used incompatible data formats. The simultaneous, distributed search was possible because clients and servers agreed on a standard document addressing scheme and adopted a common communications protocol that accommodated all the data types and formats used by the servers. Communication with other wide-area services using different protocols was accomplished by routing through so-called gateways capable of protocol translation.

The architecture of a typical networked information system from the early 1990s is shown in the diagram on page 75. Several representative clients are shown: a "dumb" terminal (that is, a terminal with no internal processor), a personal computer (PC), a Macintosh (Mac), and a NeXT machine (a computer workstation developed for use in universities and businesses, but no longer in use).

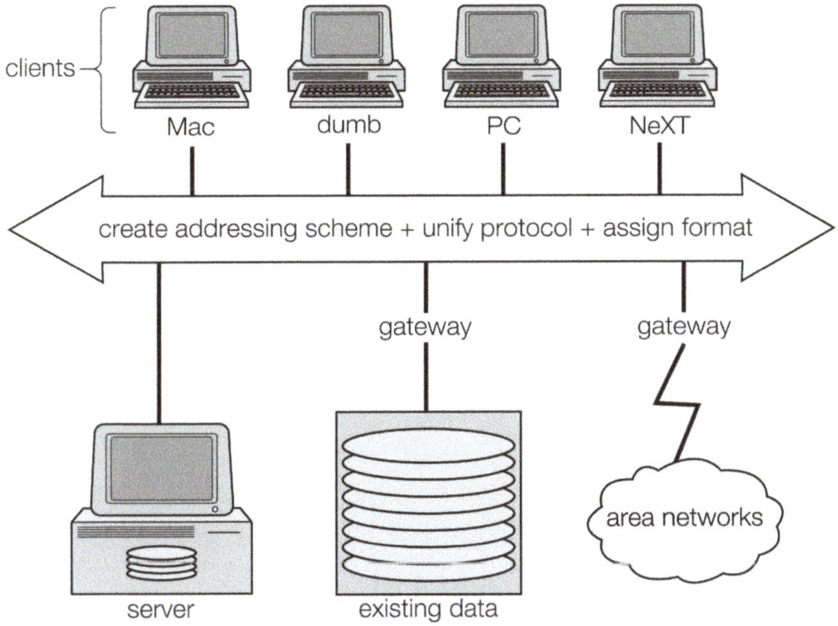

An illustration depicts the architecture of a common networked information system from the early 1990s. A "dumb" terminal that has no internal processor, a PC, a Mac, and a NeXT computer workstation are shown in this network.

Information Display

For humans to perceive and understand information, it must be presented as print and image on film or computer screen; as sound via radio or telephony; as print, sound, and video in motion pictures, on television broadcasts, or at lectures and conferences; or in face-to-face encounters. Except for live encounters and audio information, such displays emanate increasingly from digitally stored data, with the output media being video, print, and sound.

VIDEO

Possibly the most widely used video display device, at least in the industrialized world, is the television set. Designed primarily for video and sound, its image resolution generally was inadequate for alphanumeric data except in relatively small amounts. The television, computer, and communications technologies are, however, converging in a high-resolution digital television set capable of receiving alphanumeric, video, and audio signals.

The computer screen is today's ubiquitous interface that transforms computer-stored data into a form for human viewing. The two basic apparatuses used since the advent of personal computers were the cathode-ray tube (CRT) and the flat-panel display. In CRT displays an electron gun emits beams of electrons on a phosphorus-coated surface; the beams are deflected, forming visible patterns representative of data. In the first decade of the 21st century, CRTs were largely superseded by digital flat-panel displays. Advanced video display systems enable the user to scroll, page, zoom (change the scale of the details of the display image for enhancement), divide the screen into multiple colors and windows (viewing areas), and in some cases even activate commands by touching the screen instead of using the keyboard. The information capacity of the screen depends on its resolution, which ranges from low (character-addressable) to high (bit-addressable). High resolution is indispensable for the display of graphic and video data in state-of-the-art workstations, such as those used in engineering or information systems design.

Print

Modern society continues to be dominated by printed information. The generation of paper print has changed considerably, however. Although manual typesetting is still practiced for artwork, in special situations, and in some developing countries, electronic means of composing pages for subsequent reproduction by photoduplication and other methods has become commonplace.

Since the 1960s, volume publishing has become an automated process using large computers and high-speed printers to transfer digitally stored data on paper. The appearance of microcomputer-based publishing systems in the late 20th century proved to be another significant advance. Economical enough to allow even small organizations to become in-house publishers, these so-called desktop publishing systems were used to format text and graphics interactively on a high-resolution video screen with the aid of page-description command languages. Once a page was formatted, the entire image was transferred to an electronic printing or photocomposition device.

Printers

Computer printers are commonly divided into two general classes according to the way they produce images on paper: impact and nonimpact. In the first type, images are formed by the print mechanism making contact with the paper through an ink-coated ribbon. The dot-matrix printer is an example of an impact printer.

Most nonimpact printers employ different techniques for transferring images to paper. The most popular type, the laser printer, uses a beam of laser light and a system of optical components to etch images on a photoconductor drum from which they are carried via electrostatic photocopying to paper. Light-emitting diode (LED) printers resemble laser printers in operation but direct light from energized diodes rather than a laser onto a photoconductive surface. Ion-deposition printers make use of technology similar to that of photocopiers for producing electrostatic images. Another type of nonimpact printer, the ink-jet printer, sprays electrically charged drops of ink onto the print surface.

Microfilm and Microfiche

Alphanumeric and image information can be transferred from digital computer storage directly to film. Reel microfilm and microfiche (a flat sheet of film containing multiple microimages reduced from the original) were popular methods of document storage and reproduction for several decades. During the 1990s they were largely replaced by optical disc technology.

Voice

In synthetic speech generation, digitally prestored sound elements are converted to analog sound signals and combined to form words and sentences through the use of digital-to-analog converters. Human speech is the most effective natural form of communication, and so applications of this technology are becoming increasingly popular in situations where there are numerous requests for specific information (e.g., time, travel, and entertainment), where there is a need for repetitive instruction, in electronic voice mail, and in toys.

DISSEMINATION OF INFORMATION

The process of recording information by handwriting was obviously laborious and required the dedication of the likes of Egyptian scribes or monks in monasteries around the world. It was only after mechanical means of reproducing writing were invented that information records could be duplicated more efficiently and economically.

The first practical method of reproducing writing mechanically was block printing; it was developed in China during the T'ang dynasty (618–907). Ideographic text and illustrations were engraved in wooden blocks, inked, and copied on paper. Used to produce books as well as cards, charms, and calendars, block printing spread to Korea and Japan but apparently not to the Islamic or European Christian civilizations. European woodcuts and metal engravings date only to the 14th century.

Printing from movable type was also invented in China (in the mid-11th century).

There and in the bookmaking industry of Korea, where the method was applied more extensively during the 15th century, the ideographic type was made initially of baked clay and wood and later of metal. The large number of typefaces required for pictographic text composition continued to handicap printing in Asia until the present time.

The invention of character-oriented printing from movable type (1440–50) is attributed to the German printer Johannes Gutenberg. Within 30 years of his invention, the movable-type printing press was in use throughout Europe. Character-type pieces were metallic and apparently cast from metallic molds; paper and vellum (calfskin parchment) were used to carry the impressions. Gutenberg's technique of assembling individual letters by hand was employed until 1886, when the German born American printer Ottmar Mergenthaler developed the Linotype, a keyboard-driven device that cast lines of type automatically. Typesetting speed was further enhanced by the Monotype technique, in which a perforated paper ribbon, punched from a keyboard, was used to operate a type-casting machine.

Mechanical methods of typesetting prevailed until the 1960s. Since that time they have been largely supplanted by the electronic and optical printing techniques described in the previous section.

Unlike the use of movable type for printing text, early graphics were reproduced from wood relief engravings in which the nonprinting portions of the image were cut away. Musical scores, on the other hand, were reproduced from etched stone plates. At the end of the 18th century, the German printer Aloys Senefelder developed lithography, a planographic technique of transferring images from a specially prepared surface of stone. In offset lithography the image is transferred from zinc or aluminum plates instead of stone, and in photoengraving such plates are superimposed with film and then etched.

The first successful photographic process, the daguerreotype, was developed during the 1830s. The invention of photography, aside from providing a new medium for capturing still images and later video in analog form, was significant for two other reasons. First, recorded information (textual and graphic) could be easily reproduced from film, and, second, the image could be enlarged or reduced. Document reproduction from film to film has been relatively unimportant, because both printing and photocopying are cheaper. The ability to reduce images, however, has led to the development of the microform, the most economical method of disseminating analog-form information.

Another technique of considerable commercial importance for the duplication of paper-based information is photocopying, or dry photography. Printing is most economical when large numbers of copies are required, but photocopying provides a fast and efficient means of duplicating records in small quantities for personal or local use. Of the several technologies that are in use, the most popular process, xerography, is based on electrostatics.

While the volume of information issued in the form of printed matter continues unabated, the electronic publishing industry disseminates much information in digital form. The digital optical disc is a popular means of issuing large bodies of archival information, such as legislation, court and hospital records, encyclopedias and other reference works, referral databases, and libraries of computer software. Full-text databases, each containing digital page images of the complete text of some 400 periodicals stored on CD-ROM, entered the market in 1990.

The coupling of computers and digital telecommunications has also changed the modes of information dissemination. High-speed digital satellite communications facilitate electronic printing at remote sites; for example, the world's major newspapers and magazines transmit electronic page copies to different geographic locations for local printing and distribution. Updates of catalogs, computer software, and archival databases are distributed via e-mail.

Indeed, a large-scale transformation is taking place in modes of formal as well as informal communication. For more than three centuries, formal communication in the scientific community has relied on the scholarly and professional periodical, widely distributed to tens of thousands of libraries and to tens of millions of individual subscribers. In 1992 a major international publisher announced that its journals would gradually be available for computer storage in digital form; and in that same year the State University of New York at Buffalo began building a completely electronic, paperless library. The scholarly article, rather than the journal, is likely to become the basic unit of formal communication in scientific disciplines; digital copies of such an article will be transmitted electronically to subscribers or, more likely, on demand to individuals and organizations who learn of its existence through referral databases and new types of alerting information services. The Internet already offers instantaneous public access to vast resources of noncommercial information stored in computers around the world.

Similarly, the traditional modes of informal communications—various types of face-to-face encounters such as meetings, conferences, seminars, workshops, and classroom lectures—are being supplemented and in some cases replaced by e-mail, texting, social media, teleconferencing, virtual meetings, and groupware. These technologies are forging virtual societal networks—communities of geographically dispersed individuals who have common professional or social interests.

CHAPTER 4

INFORMATION AND LIBRARIES

Printed books and periodicals have long been collected, preserved, stored, and made ready for use in libraries. In the 20th century libraries also became major collectors of maps, prints and photographs, reproductions of printed materials (such as on microfilm), recorded sound and moving images, and even artifacts. Now libraries are also a gateway to enormous quantities of information from computer databases.

For example, a library patron can read United States President John F. Kennedy's inaugural address—containing the famous words, "ask not what your country can do for you; ask what you can do for your country"—from a microfilm of a newspaper published on January 21, 1961. Alternatively, the patron can be inspired by the speech as reproduced in a collection of historical documents, either in a book, on a computer disk, or online. The library may also own an audio or video recording of the speech or provide access to one via the Internet.

Libraries provide the means by which people can obtain knowledge. Students can gain access to countless resources and vast amounts of information through a library's collections and databases.

INFORMATION TECHNOLOGY AND LIBRARIES

The quantity of information libraries have to deal with is ever increasing. Modern librarians have adopted new technologies to meet the needs of their users.

In the 1930s storing back issues of newspapers was a major problem for libraries. The files bulked large in the stacks, the volumes were unwieldy, and the brittle newsprint fell apart

The Librarian as Information Scientist

A librarian is a mover of information from one person to another. Having library skills is not enough. A librarian should also understand the bigger picture via information science, of which library science is just one part. To teach the use of a library, a librarian must understand how people think when they attack research problems. To construct an index, a librarian must understand how language works. These tasks and more are part of information science, and in fact, many librarians today are called information scientists.

A librarian, also called an information specialist, frequently specializes in certain subject areas. Librarians need to understand the nature of information and how to make it accessible to patrons.

A librarian must keep up with the latest innovations in computer technology and database management. To run a library, the librarian must learn techniques for analyzing and improving a system. Information science includes systems analysis, too.

The various branches of the information profession share many objectives, practices, and skills. Each branch works to make the records of human progress readily available, and the contribution of each to society can only suffer from the lack of integration into a larger whole. Librarians often specialize in certain areas. Their professional skills range from those of the archivist, who is concerned with records management, records appraisal, accessioning and arrangement, archival buildings and storage facilities, preservation and rehabilitation, and reference services (including exhibition and publication), to those of the information scientist, who is concerned with research on the nature of information itself and the process of information flow and transfer between individuals and communities.

The personnel requirements of the profession include several categories, based on various kinds of specialist knowledge and skills. These include a knowledge of the nature of documents and their role in collection building, skills in the organization of knowledge through cataloging and classification, an ability to analyze and survey needs and to disseminate information in response to and in advance of inquiries, and, often, a high level of computer literacy. Support personnel are needed to maintain the equipment, both hardware and software, and clerks, technicians, and stewards also are essential.

when handled. The problem was solved with photographic technology. Preserved on spools of microfilm, a year's worth of even the fattest newspaper could fit into a single file drawer. Unique items such as university Ph.D. dissertations also were disseminated on microfilm. Microfiche, introduced later, provided handier access to such items as reports and books. One microfiche can hold up to 1,000 pages of a book, and an ultrafiche can hold up to 3,000 pages. (In addition, acidic paper, which deteriorates rapidly, has been widely used for many years not only for newspapers but also for books and magazines. Librarians have taken the lead in developing chemical deacidification processes and in encouraging publishers to use acid-free paper.)

The installation of fax (facsimile transmission) machines in libraries played a major role in speeding document delivery. Plain-paper photocopying came to libraries in the early 1960s and is still widely used, both by the public and by librarians filling interlibrary loan requests for magazine articles and the like. The fair-use provisions of copyright law allow some photocopying and exchanging of photocopies among libraries or users.

Computer technology has helped libraries to organize and disseminate an even greater quantity of information. Starting in the 1980s, CD–ROM technology revolutionized the way information is stored, accessed, and retrieved. The DVD–ROM (digital video disc–read only memory), introduced in the 1990s, has a much greater storage capacity than the CD–ROM, allowing both a greater amount and a higher quality of text and multimedia content to be stored on one disc.

Starting in the last three decades of the 20th century, the amount of information stored on computers around the world increased dramatically. Through the Internet and the rise of personal computers, much of this information is now accessible to individual users in their homes, as well as in libraries.

Online databases came into wide use in the 1970s. One of the first was Medline, which the National Library of Medicine made available in 1971. Dialog, originally developed by the Lockheed Aircraft Corporation, became available to the public in 1972. Lexis, a database for lawyers, started in 1973, while Nexis, more general in scope, began in 1979; the two later merged. Online databases like Dialog and LexisNexis provided fee-paying subscribers with access to many kinds of reports, documents, and articles from journals and newspapers. Without the assistance of a

The National Library of Medicine's Medline was one of the first online databases to be used extensively. MedlinePlus provides medical and health information to people using a variety of digital devices.

skilled researcher, however, it was difficult to use these databases cost-effectively.

By the beginning of the 21st century, online search engines such as Google had become valuable information resources. Without paying a fee, anyone with Internet access could type in a topic at such a search engine and almost instantly gain access to thousands of potentially relevant Web sites, ranked in such a way that the most useful were usually displayed first. So easy was the process that many computer users were tempted to bypass libraries entirely for purposes of research. Librarians and others hastened to point out that such a computer user was missing out on the so-called "deep Web" of statistical, bibliographical, and other databases that were not fully accessible through the search engines. They also were ready to remind such people that a vast quantity of recorded knowledge had not yet been scanned onto the Internet. Still another issue was reliability of data—numerous Web sites, unlike traditional publishers, were open to new postings almost without restriction. Help with all these issues, however, can be obtained from a professional librarian.

THE CHANGING ROLE OF LIBRARIES

Libraries were involved early in exploiting information technologies. For many years libraries have participated in cooperative ventures with other libraries. Different institutions have shared cataloging and information about what each has in its collection. They have used this shared information to facilitate the borrowing and lending of materials among libraries. Librarians have also become expert in finding information from online and electronic databases.

As society has begun to value information more highly, the so-called information industry has developed. This industry encompasses publishers, software developers, online information services, and other businesses that package and sell information products for a profit. It provides both an opportunity and a challenge to libraries. On the one hand, as more information becomes available in electronic form, libraries no longer have to own an article or a certain piece of statistical information in order to obtain it quickly for a user. On the other hand, members of the information industry seem to be offering alternatives to libraries. A student with her own computer can now go directly to an online service to locate, order, and receive a copy of an article without ever leaving her home.

Although the development of digital libraries means that people do not have to go to a building for some kinds of information, users still need help to locate the information they want. In a traditional library building, a user has access to a catalog that will help locate a book. In a digital library, a user has access to catalogs to find traditional library materials, but much of the information on, for example, the Internet can not be found through one commonly accepted form of identification. This problem necessitates agreement on standard ways to identify pieces of electronic information (sometimes called meta-data) and the development of codes (such as HTML [Hypertext Markup Language] and SGML [Standard Generalized Markup Language]) that can be inserted into electronic texts.

For many years libraries have bought books and periodicals that people can borrow or photocopy for personal use. Publishers of electronic databases, however, do not usually sell their product; instead, they license it to libraries (or sites) for specific uses. They usually charge libraries a per-user fee or a per-unit fee for the specific amount of information the library uses. When libraries do not own these resources, they have less control over whether older information is saved for future use—another important cultural function of libraries. In the electronic age, questions of copyright, intellectual property rights, and the economics of information have become increasingly important to the future of library service.

Increased availability of electronic information has led libraries, particularly in schools, colleges, and universities, to develop important relationships to their institutions' computer centers. In some places the computer center is the place responsible

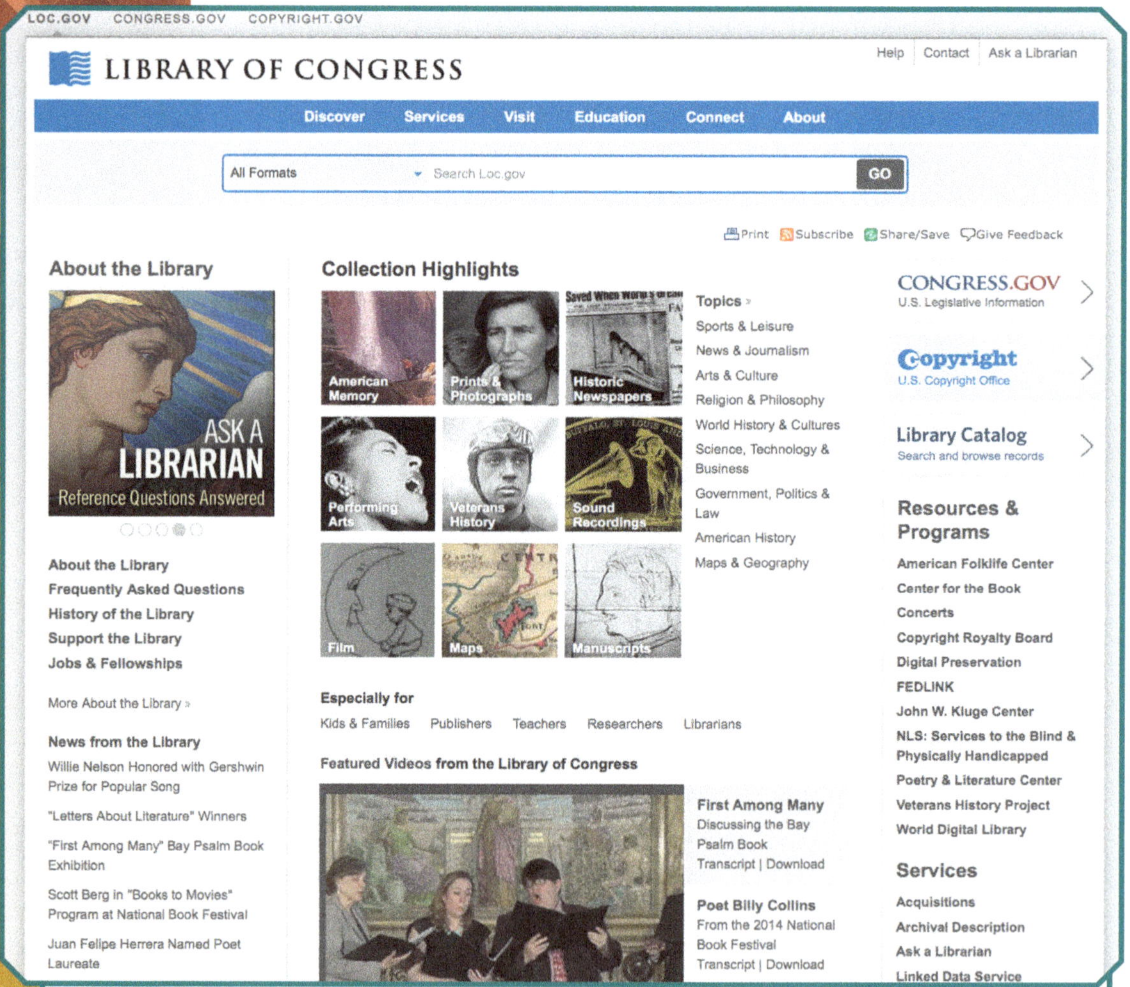

The online catalog of the Library of Congress (LOC) contains nearly 18 million records describing the LOC's collections. Users can search records by keyword or browse by author/creator, subject, name/title, uniform title, and call number.

for electronic information and the library is responsible for print information. In some educational institutions, librarians have assumed responsibility for both the library collection and computer services.

As technology has changed and allowed ever new ways of creating, storing, organizing, and providing information, public expectation of the role of libraries has increased. Libraries have responded by developing more sophisticated online catalogs that allow users to find out whether or not a book has been checked out and what other libraries have it. Libraries have also found that users want information faster, they want the full text of a document instead of a citation to it, and they want information that clearly answers their questions. In response, libraries have provided Selective Dissemination of Information (SDI) services, in which librarians choose information that may be of interest to their users and forward it to them before the users request it.

The changes in libraries described here originated in the United States and other English-speaking countries. But electronic networks do not have geographic boundaries, and their influence has spread rapidly. With Internet connections in Beijing, Moscow, and across the globe, people who did not have access to traditional library services now have the opportunity to get information about all types of subjects, free of political censorship.

As libraries have changed, so, too, has the role of the librarian. Increasingly librarians have assumed the role of educator to teach their users how to find information both in the library and over electronic networks. Public librarians have expanded their roles by providing local community information through publicly accessible computing systems. Some librarians are experts about computers and computer software. Others are concerned with how computer technologies can preserve the human cultural records of the past or assure that library collections on crumbling paper or in old computer files can still be used by people many centuries in the future.

The work of librarians has also moved outside library walls. Librarians have begun to work in the information industry as salespeople, designers of new information systems, researchers, and information analysts. They also are found in such fields as marketing and public relations and in such organizations as law firms, where staffs need rapid access to information.

Although libraries have changed significantly over the course of history, their cultural role has not. Libraries remain responsible for acquiring or providing access to books, periodicals, and other media that meet the educational, recreational, and informational needs of their users. They continue to keep the business, legal, historical, and religious records of a civilization. They are the place where a toddler can hear his first story and a scholar can carry out her research.

CHAPTER 5

ORGANIZATIONAL CONTROL AND DISSEMINATION OF INFORMATION

An information system is an integrated set of components for collecting, storing, and processing data and for delivering information, knowledge, and digital products. Business firms and other organizations rely on information systems to carry out and manage their operations, interact with their customers and suppliers, and compete in the marketplace. For instance, corporations use information systems to reach their potential customers with targeted messages over the Web, to process financial accounts, and to manage their human resources. Governments deploy information systems to provide services cost-effectively to citizens. Digital goods, such as electronic books and software, and online services, such as auctions and social networking, are delivered with information systems. Individuals rely on information systems, generally Internet-based, for conducting much of their personal lives: for socializing, study, shopping, banking, and entertainment.

As major new technologies for recording and processing information have been invented over the millennia, new capabilities have appeared. The invention of the printing press by Johannes Gutenberg in the mid-15th century and the invention of a mechanical calculator by Blaise Pascal in the 17th century are but two examples. These inventions led to a profound revolution in the ability to record, process, and disseminate information and knowledge. The first large-scale mechanical information system was Herman Hollerith's census tabulator. Invented in time to process thc 1890 U.S. census, Hollerith's machine represented a major step in automation, as well as an inspiration to develop computerized information systems.

Johannes Gutenberg's movable type enabled a large number of books to be printed quickly, which led to the spread of knowledge.

One of the first computers used for such information processing was the UNIVAC I, installed at the U.S. Bureau of the Census in 1951 for administrative use and at General Electric in 1954 for commercial use. Beginning in the late 1970s, personal computers brought some of the advantages of information systems to small businesses and to individuals. Early in the same decade the Internet began its expansion as the global network of networks. In 1991 the World Wide Web, invented by Tim Berners-Lee as a means to access the interlinked information stored in the computers connected by the Internet, was installed to become the principal service delivered on the network.

Tim Berners-Lee invented the World Wide Web in 1991. The Web gives users access to a vast array of documents that are connected to each other by means of hypertext or hyperlinks, allowing users easy access to them.

The global penetration of the Internet and the Web has enabled access to information and other resources and facilitated the forming of relationships among people and organizations on an unprecedented scale. The progress of electronic commerce over the Internet has resulted in a dramatic growth in digital interpersonal communications (via e-mail and social networks), distribution of products (software, music, e-books, and movies), and business transactions (buying, selling, and advertising on the Web). With the emergence of smartphones, tablets, and other computer-based mobile devices, all connected by wireless communication networks, information systems have been extended to support mobility as the natural human condition.

As information systems have enabled more diverse human activities, they have exerted a profound influence over society. These systems have quickened the pace of daily activities, affected the structure and mix of organizations, changed the type of products bought, and influenced the nature of work. Information and knowledge have become vital economic resources. Yet, along with opportunities, the dependence on information systems has brought new threats. Intensive industry innovation and academic research continually develop new opportunities while aiming to contain the threats.

COMPONENTS OF INFORMATION SYSTEMS

The main components of information systems are computer hardware and software, telecommunications, databases and data warehouses, human resources, and procedures. The hardware, software, and telecommunications constitute information technology (IT), which is now ingrained in the operations and management of organizations.

COMPUTER HARDWARE

Today even the smallest firms, as well as many households throughout the world, own or lease computers. These are usually microcomputers, also called personal computers. Individuals may own multiple computers in the form of smartphones and other portable devices. Large organizations typically employ distributed computer systems, from powerful parallel-processing servers located in data centers to widely dispersed personal computers and mobile devices, integrated into the organizational information systems.

These computer technicians are working in a server room. Many organizations and businesses have computer systems and servers that are situated in centralized storehouses called data centers.

Together with the peripheral equipment, such as magnetic or solid-state storage disks, input-output devices, and telecommunications gear, these constitute the hardware of information systems.

The cost of hardware has steadily and rapidly decreased, while processing speed and storage capacity have increased vastly. However, hardware's use of electric power and its environmental impact are concerns being addressed by computer systems designers.

COMPUTER SOFTWARE

Computer software falls into two broad classes: system software and application software. The principal system software is the operating system. It manages the hardware, data and program files, and other system resources and provides means for the user to control the computer, generally via a graphical user interface (GUI). Application software is programs designed to handle specific tasks for users. Examples include general-purpose application suites with their spreadsheet and

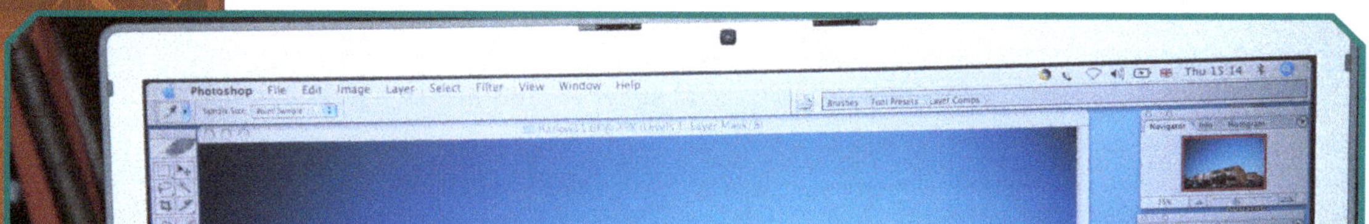

Adobe Photoshop is a software program that enables a user to edit images. It is sometimes called a paint program because it allows graphic designers to draw pictures on a display screen by using special tools, such as painting, pen, or brush tools.

word-processing programs, as well as "vertical" applications that serve a specific industry segment—for instance, an application that schedules, routes, and tracks package deliveries for an overnight carrier. Larger firms use licensed applications, customizing them to meet their specific needs, and develop other applications in-house or on an outsourced basis. Companies may also use applications delivered as software-as-a-service (SaaS) over the Web. Proprietary software, available from and supported by its vendors, is being challenged by open-source software available on the Web for free use and modification under a license that protects its future availability.

Cloud computing is a method of running application software and storing related data in central computer systems and providing customers or other users access to them through the Internet. Cloud-computing companies either charge users for their services, through subscriptions and usage fees, or provide free access to the services and charge companies for placing advertisements in the services.

Telecommunications

Telecommunications are used to connect, or network, computer systems and transmit

A wireless router is a hardware device used to connect a computer to a network for wireless networking, also known as Wi-Fi. Multiple users can share a Wi-Fi connection to the Internet, within a certain distance from the wireless signal.

information. Connections are established via wired or wireless media. Wired technologies include coaxial cable and fiber optics. Wireless technologies, predominantly based on the transmission of microwaves and radio waves, support mobile computing. Pervasive information systems have arisen with the computing devices embedded in many different physical objects. For example, sensors such as radio frequency identification devices (RFIDs) can be attached to products moving through the supply chain to enable the tracking of their location and the monitoring of their condition. Wireless sensor networks that are integrated into the Internet can produce massive amounts of data that can be used in seeking higher productivity or in monitoring the environment.

Various computer network configurations are possible, depending on the needs of an organization. Local area networks (LANs) join computers at a particular site, such as an office building or an academic campus. Metropolitan area networks (MANs) cover a limited densely populated area. Wide area networks (WANs) connect widely distributed data centers, frequently run by different organizations. The Internet is a network of networks, connecting billions of computers located on every continent. Through networking, users gain access to information resources, such as large databases, and to other individuals, such as coworkers, clients, or people who share their professional or private interests. Internet-type services can be provided within an organization and for its exclusive use by various intranets that are accessible through a browser; for example, an intranet may be deployed as an access portal to a shared corporate document base. To connect with business partners over the Internet in a private and secure manner, extranets are established as so-called virtual private networks (VPNs) by encrypting the messages.

DATABASES AND DATA WAREHOUSES

Many information systems are primarily delivery vehicles for data stored in databases, which support the operations and management functions of an enterprise. Data warehouses contain the archival data, collected over time, that can be mined for information in order to develop and market new products, serve the existing customers better, or reach out to potential new customers. Anyone who has ever purchased something with a credit card—in

Data warehouses usually contain thousands of server computers networked together. They provide secure storage of electronic data and an easy way to manage and retrieve data.

person, by mail order, or over the Web—is included within such data collections.

Construction of the large data centers that run cloud-computing services often requires investments of hundreds of millions of dollars. The centers typically contain thousands of server computers networked together into parallel-processing or grid-computing systems. The centers also often employ sophisticated virtualization technologies, which allow computer systems to be divided into many virtual machines that can be rented temporarily to

CLOUD COMPUTING

Cloud computing is increasingly being adopted as a source of information services. It offers on-demand access to data via the Internet to services furnished by a provider that runs data centers with the necessary software. The services can be provided at one of three levels: as the infrastructure for running existing applications, as the platform for developing new applications, or as software-as-a-service (SaaS) to be used by the firm over the network. In particular, SaaS has become a cost-effective way to use enterprise systems. Generally, cloud computing is provided by external vendors (such as Google Drive), though some firms implement their own private clouds to share resources and access them over the network. Scalability and avoidance of capital expenditures are notable advantages of public clouds; the partial loss of control is a drawback.

customers. Because of their intensive use of electricity, the centers are often located near hydroelectric dams or other sources of cheap and plentiful electric power.

Because cloud computing involves the storage of often sensitive personal or commercial information in central database systems run by third parties, it raises concerns about data privacy and security as well as the transmission of data across national boundaries. It also stirs fears about the eventual creation of data monopolies. Some believe that cloud computing will, like other public utilities, come to be heavily regulated by governments.

Managing Information Systems

For an organization to use its information services to launch a new initiative, those services have to be part of a well-planned infrastructure of core resources. Many organizations rely on outside firms—that is, specialized IT companies—to deliver some, or even all, of their information services. If located in-house, the management of information systems can be decentralized to a certain degree to correspond to the organization's overall structure.

Information System Infrastructure and Architecture

A well-designed information system rests on a coherent foundation that supports responsive change—and, thus, the organization's agility—as new business or administrative initiatives arise. Known as the information system infrastructure, the foundation consists of core telecommunications networks, databases and data warehouses, software, hardware, and procedures managed by various specialists. With business globalization, an organization's infrastructure often crosses many national boundaries. Establishing and maintaining a complex infrastructure requires extensive planning and consistent implementation to handle strategic corporate affairs.

When organized into a coherent whole, the specific information systems that support operations, management, and knowledge work constitute the system architecture of an organization. Clearly, an organization's long-term general strategic plans must be considered when designing an information system infrastructure and architecture.

ORGANIZATION OF INFORMATION SERVICES

An information services unit is typically in charge of an organization's information systems. When the systems are largely outsourced, this unit is of a limited size and concentrates on aligning the systems with the corporate competitive strategy and on supervising the outside company's services. When information services are provided in-house and centralized, this unit is responsible for planning, acquiring,

A director of security information systems watches a company's security operations center. Many companies and organizations have a chief information officer who is responsible for all aspects of information services, including security.

operating, and maintaining information systems for the entire organization. In decentralized structures, however, the central unit is responsible only for planning and maintaining the infrastructure, while business and administrative specialists supervise systems and services for their own units. A variety of intermediate organizational forms are possible.

In many organizations, information systems are headed by a chief information officer (CIO). The activities of information services are usually supervised by a steering committee;

in an organization where information systems play a strategic role, the board of directors need to be involved in their governance.

INFORMATION SYSTEMS SECURITY AND CONTROL

With the opening of information systems to the global Internet and with their thorough infusion into the operation and management of business and government organizations and into the infrastructure of daily life across the world, security issues have moved to the forefront of concerns about global well-being.

INFORMATION SYSTEMS SECURITY

Information systems security is responsible for the integrity and safety of system resources and activities. Most organizations in developed countries are dependent on the secure operation of their information systems. In fact, the very fabric of societies often depends on this security. Information systems are at the heart of intensive care units and air traffic control systems. Financial institutions could not survive a total failure of their information systems for longer than a day or two. Electronic funds transfer systems (EFTS) handle immense amounts of money that exist only as electronic signals sent over the networks or as magnetized spots on storage disks. Information systems are vulnerable to a number of threats, which require strict controls such as countermeasures and regular audits to ensure that the system remains secure.

Although instances of computer crime and abuse receive extensive media attention, human error is estimated to cause greater losses in information systems operation.

In 2015 after a data breach in the U.S. Office of Personnel Management, top officials, including chief information officers, testified about the breach before a committee of the House of Representatives on Capitol Hill in Washington, D.C.

Disasters such as earthquakes, floods, and fires are the particular concern of disaster recovery planning, which is a part of a corporate business continuity plan. A contingency scheme is also necessary to cover the failure of servers, telecommunications networks, or software.

COMPUTER CRIME AND ABUSE

Computer crime—illegal acts in which computers are the primary tool—costs the world economy billions of dollars annually. Computer abuse does not rise to the level of crime, yet it involves unethical use of a computer. The objectives of the so-called hacking of information systems include vandalism, theft of consumer information, governmental and commercial espionage, sabotage, and cyberwar. Some of the more widespread means of computer crime include phishing and planting of malware, such as computer viruses and worms, Trojan horses, and logic bombs.

Phishing involves obtaining a legitimate user's login and other information by subterfuge with messages fraudulently claiming to originate with a legitimate entity, such as a bank or government office. A successful phishing raid to obtain a user's information may be followed by identity theft, an impersonation of the user to gain access to the user's resources.

Computer viruses are a particularly common form of attack. These are program instructions that are able not only to perform malicious acts but also to insert copies of themselves into other programs and thus spread to other computer systems. Similar to viruses are worms, complete computer programs that replicate through telecommunications networks. Because of their ability to spread rapidly and widely, viruses and worms can inflict immense damage. The damage can be in the form of tampering with system operation, theft of large volumes of data (e.g., credit card numbers), or denial of service by overloading systems with a barrage of spurious requests.

In a Trojan horse attack, the malefactor conceals unauthorized instructions within an authorized program. A logic bomb consists of hidden instructions, often introduced with the Trojan horse technique, that stay dormant until a specific event occurs, at which time the instructions are activated. In one well-known case, in 1985 a programmer at an insurance company in Fort Worth, Texas, placed a logic bomb in his company's human resources system; when he was fired and his name was deleted from the company's employee database, the entire database was erased.

Once a system connected to the Internet is invaded, it may be used to take over many others and organize them into so-called botnets that can launch massive attacks against other systems to steal information or sabotage their operation.

INFORMATION SYSTEMS CONTROLS

To ensure secure and efficient operation of information systems, an organization institutes a set of procedures and technological measures called controls. Information systems are safeguarded through a combination of general and application controls.

General controls apply to information system activities throughout an organization. The most important general controls are the measures that control access to computer systems and the information stored there or transmitted over telecommunications networks. General controls include administrative measures that restrict employees' access to only those processes directly relevant to their duties. As a result, these controls limit the damage that any individual can do. Fault-tolerant computer systems installed in critical environments, such as in hospital information systems or securities marketplaces, are designed to control and isolate problems so that the system can continue to function.

Application controls are specific to a given application and include such measures as validating input data, logging the accesses to the system, regularly archiving copies of various databases, and ensuring that information is disseminated only to authorized users.

Securing Information

Controlling access to information systems became profoundly more difficult with the spread of wide-area networks (WANs) and, in particular, the Internet. Users, as well as interlopers, may access systems from any unattended computer within an organization or from virtually anywhere over the Internet. As a security measure, each legitimate user has a unique name and a regularly changed password. Another security measure is to require some form of physical authentication, such as an object (a physical token or a smart card) or a personal characteristic (fingerprint, retinal pattern, hand geometry, or signature). Many systems combine these types of measures—such as automatic teller machines, which rely on a combination of a personal identification number (PIN) and an identification card. Security measures placed between an organization's internal networks and the Internet are known as firewalls.

A different way to prohibit access to information is via data encryption, which has gained particular importance in electronic commerce. Public key encryption is used widely in such commerce. To ensure confidentiality, only the intended addressee has the private key needed to decrypt messages that have been encrypted with the addressee's public key. Furthermore, authentication of both parties in an electronic transaction is possible through the digital certificates issued to both parties by a trusted third party and the use of digital signatures—an additional code attached to the message to verify its origin. A type of antitampering code can also be attached to a message to detect corruption. Similar means are available to ensure that parties to an electronic transaction cannot later repudiate their participation. Some messages require additional attributes. For example, electronic cash is a type of message, with encryption used to ensure the purchaser's anonymity, that acts like physical cash.

To continually monitor information systems, intrusion detection systems are used.

They detect anomalous events and log the information necessary to produce reports and to establish the source and the nature of the possible intrusion. More active systems also attempt to prevent the intrusion upon detection.

Information Systems Audit

The effectiveness of an information system's controls is evaluated through an information systems audit. An audit aims to establish whether information systems are safeguarding corporate assets, maintaining the integrity of data, supporting corporate objectives effectively, and operating efficiently. It is a part of a more general financial audit that verifies an organization's accounting records and financial statements. Information systems are designed so that every financial transaction can be traced. In other words, an audit trail must exist that can establish where each transaction originated and how it was processed. Aside from financial audits, operational audits are used to evaluate the effectiveness and efficiency of information systems operations, and technological audits verify that information technologies are appropriately chosen, configured, and implemented.

CONCLUSION

Along with the global transportation infrastructure, network-based information systems have been a factor in the growth of international business and corporations. A relationship between the deployment of information systems and higher productivity has been shown in a number of industries when these systems complement other corporate resources. Electronic commerce has moved many relationships and transactions among companies and individuals to the Internet and the Web, with the resulting expansion of possibilities and efficiencies. The development of the Web-based environment, accompanied by the low cost of hardware and telecommunications and the availability of open-source software, has led to a flowering of entrepreneurial activity and the emergence to prominence and significant market value of numerous firms based on new business models.

As the use of information systems has become pervasive in advanced economies and societies at large, several societal and ethical issues have moved into the forefront.

The most important are issues of individual privacy, property rights, universal access and free speech, information accuracy, and quality of life.

Individual privacy hinges on the right to control one's personal information. While invasion of privacy is generally perceived as an undesirable loss of autonomy, government and business organizations do need to collect data in order to facilitate administration and exploit marketing opportunities. Electronic commerce presents a particular challenge to privacy, as personal information is routinely collected and disseminated in a largely unregulated manner. The ownership of and control over the personal profiles, contacts, and communications in social networks are one example of a privacy issue that awaits resolution through a combination of

Protecting personal information is very important to users of electronic devices in free Wi-Fi spots or on public computers.

market forces, industry self-regulation, and possibly government regulation. Preventing invasions of privacy is complicated by the lack of an international legal standard.

Intellectual property, such as software, books, music, and movies, is protected, albeit imperfectly, by patents, trade secrets, and copyrights. However, such intangible goods can be easily copied and transmitted electronically over the Web for unlawful reproduction and use. Combinations of legal statutes and technological safeguards, including antipiracy encryption and electronic watermarks, are in place, but much of the abuse prevention relies on the ethics of the user.

Access to information systems over the Web is necessary for full participation in modern society. In particular, it is desirable to avoid the emergence of digital divides between nations or regions and between social and ethnic groups. Open access to the Web as a medium for human communication and as a repository for shared knowledge is treasured. Indeed, many people consider free speech a universal human right and the Internet and Web the most widely accessible means to exercise this right. Yet, legitimate concerns arise about protecting children without resorting to censorship. Technological solutions, such as software that filters out pornography and inappropriate communications, are partially successful.

Of concern to everyone is the accuracy and security of information contained in databases and data warehouses—whether in health and insurance data, credit bureau records, or government files—as misinformation or privileged information released inappropriately can adversely affect personal safety, livelihood, and everyday life. Individuals must cooperate in reviewing and correcting their files, and organizations must ensure appropriate security, access, and use of such files.

Information systems have affected the quality of personal and working lives. In the workplace, information systems can be deployed to eliminate tedious tasks and give workers greater autonomy, or they can be used to thoughtlessly eliminate jobs and subject the remaining workforce to pervasive electronic surveillance. Consumers can use the Web for shopping, networking, and entertainment—but at the risk of contending with spam (unsolicited e-mail), interception of credit card numbers, and attack by computer viruses.

Information systems can expand participation of ordinary citizens in government through electronic elections, referendums, and polls, and can also provide electronic access to government services and information—permitting, for instance, electronic filing of taxes, direct deposit of government checks, and viewing of current and historical government documents. More transparent and beneficial government operations are possible by opening the data collected by and about governments to public scrutiny in a searchable and easy-to-use form. With the Web, the public sphere of deliberation and self-organization can expand and give voice to individuals. However, information systems have also conjured Orwellian images of government surveillance and business intrusion into private lives. It remains for society to harness the power of information systems by strengthening the legal, social, and technological elements involved.

abstract A summary of points (as of a writing) usually presented in skeletal form; something that summarizes or concentrates the essentials of a larger thing or several things.

alphanumeric Consisting of both letters and numbers.

analog computer A computer that works with numbers represented by directly measurable quantities (as voltages or resistances).

autonomy Self-directing freedom and especially moral independence; a self-governing state.

binary digit Either of the two digits, conventionally 0 and 1, used in a binary system of numeration; also called a bit.

byte The digital representation of a character by eight bits, or binary digits.

Boolean algebra Any of several logical systems of combining abstract quantities; an arithmetic of sets in which the intersection and union of sets are operations.

botnet A network of computers, especially those that have been linked together by malware.

catalog A list of names, titles, or articles arranged according to a system; a book or file containing a catalog; to make a catalog of.

classification The act or process of classifying; an arrangement of people or things into groups based on ways that they are alike.

cloud computing The method of running application software and storing related data in central computer systems and providing customers or other users access to them through the Internet.

cognitive Relating to or being conscious of mental activities (as thinking, reasoning, remembering, imagining, learning words, and using language).

decoder Something that changes a message from code into ordinary language.

digital computer A computer that operates with numbers expressed as digits (as in the binary system).

e-book A book composed in or converted to digital format for display on a computer screen or handheld device.

encoder A transmitter.

encryption The act of enciphering or encoding.

index A list (as of bibliographical

information or citations to a body of literature) arranged usually in alphabetical order of some specified datum (such as author, subject, or keyword); a usually alphabetical list that includes all or nearly all items (as topics, names of people and places) of special pertinence and covered or mentioned in a printed or written work, that gives with each item the place (as by page number) where it may be found in the work.

intellectual property Property (as an idea, method, or written work) that derives from the work of the mind.

logarithm The exponent or power to which a base is raised to yield a given number. Expressed mathematically, x is the logarithm of n to the base b if $b^x = n$; this is expressed by the equation $x = \log_b n$.

malware Software that has been designed to interfere with a computer's normal functioning.

parity The property of an integer with respect to being odd or even; the state of being odd or even used as the basis of a method of detecting errors in binary-coded data.

periodical A magazine or other publication of which the issues appear at stated or regular intervals—usually used of a publication appearing more frequently than annually but infrequently used of a newspaper.

semiotics A general philosophical theory of signs and symbols that deals especially with their function in both artificially constructed and natural languages and comprises the three branches of syntactics, semantics, and pragmatics.

steering committee A group of people who are in charge of managing or directing something.

FOR MORE INFORMATION

American Library Association (ALA)
50 East Huron Street
Chicago, IL 60611
(800) 545-2433
Website: http://www.ala.org
The ALA was established in 1876 to offer leadership for developing, promoting, and improving library and information services and for librarians so that they can help learning and increase access to information for everyone.

Anita Borg Institute
1501 Page Mill Road
MS 1105
Palo Alto, CA 94304
(212) 897-2157
Website: http://anitaborg.org
This organization, founded by computer scientist and researcher Anita Borg, provides encouragement and support to women in all aspects of technology.

Association for Computing Machinery (ACM)
2 Penn Plaza, Suite 701

New York, NY 10121-0701
(800) 342-6626
Website: https://www.acm.org
ACM is an educational and scientific computing society that offers resources to encourage computing as a science and a profession. It provides a digital library of articles published by ACM and sources from key computing publishers.

Association for Information Science and Technology (ASIS&T)
8555 Sixteenth Street, Suite 850
Silver Spring, MD 20910
(301) 495-0900
Website: https://www.asis.org
This organization offers support and guidance to professionals in the field of information science. It works to increase access to information and improve the methods by which society stores, retrieves, analyzes, manages, archives, and spreads information.

Canada's Association of IT Professionals (CIPS)
National Office
5090 Explorer Drive, Suite 801
Mississauga, ON L4W 4T9

Canada
(905) 602-1370
Website: http://www.cips.ca
CIPS helps to improve the Canadian IT industry by creating standards and sharing best practices among members. It also provides networking opportunities and certifies and accredits IT professionals and college programs.

Canadian Association of Computer Science (CACS)
c/o Department of Computer Science
University of Calgary
2500 University Drive NW
Calgary AB T2N 1N4
Canada
(403) 220-8497
Website: http://cacsaic.org
This Canadian organization encourages computer science research and honors outstanding young computer science researchers with annual awards.

Information Sciences Institute (ISI)
USC Viterbi School of Engineering
4676 Admiralty Way
Marina del Rey, CA
(310) 822-1511

Website: http://www.isi.edu
ISI is a leader in research and helped design the Internet, including communications protocols. It created the Domain Name System and employs engineers and research scientists to develop technologies in information processing, computers, and communications.

The Institute of Electrical and Electronics Engineers Computer Society
2001 L Street NW, Suite 700
Washington, DC 20036-4928
(202) 371-0101
Website: https://www.computer.org
This society is a leading membership organization involving computer science and technology and provides networking and career-development resources.

WEBSITES

Due to the changing nature of Internet links, Rosen Publishing has developed an online list of websites related to the subject of this book. This site is updated regularly. Please use this link to access the list:

http://www.rosenlinks.com/SCI/Info

FOR FURTHER READING

Bawden, David, and Lyn Robinson. *Introduction to Information Science.* Chicago, IL: Neal-Schuman, 2013.

Curley, Rob, ed. *Cryptography: Cracking Codes* (Intelligence and Counterintelligence). New York, NY: Britannica Educational Publishing and Rosen Educational Services, 2014.

Curley, Robert, ed. *Architects of the Information Age* (Computing and Connecting in the 21st Century). New York, NY: Britannica Educational Publishing and Rosen Educational Services, 2012.

Curley, Robert, ed. *Computing: From the Abacus to the iPad* (Computing and Connecting in the 21st Century). New York, NY: Britannica Educational Publishing and Rosen Educational Services, 2012.

Curley, Robert, ed. *Issues in Cyberspace: From Privacy to Piracy* (Computing and

Connecting in the 21st Century). New York, NY: Britannica Educational Publishing and Rosen Educational Services, 2012.

Evans, G. Edward, Sheila S. Intner, and Jean Riddle Weihs. *Introduction to Technical Services* (Library Science Text Series). Santa Barbara, CA: Libraries Unlimited, 2011.

Freedman, Jeri. *Careers in Computer Science and Programming* (Careers in Computer Technology). New York, NY: Rosen Publishing, 2011.

Goodrich, Michael T., and Roberto Tamassia. *Introduction to Computer Security*. Boston, MA: Pearson, 2011.

Haftor, Darek J., Anita Mirijamdotter, and Gunilla Bradley. *Information and Communication Technologies, Society and Human Beings: Theory and Framework*. Hershey, PA: Information Science Reference, 2011.

Laudon, Kenneth C., and Jane P. Laudon. *Management Information Systems: Managing the Digital Firm*. 14th ed. Boston, MA: Pearson, 2016.

Manning, Christopher D., Prabhakar Raghavan, and Hinrich Schütze. *Introduction to Information Retrieval.* New York, NY: Cambridge University Press, 2008.

Prentice, Ann E. *Public Libraries in the 21st Century* (Library and Information Science Text Series). Santa Barbara, CA: Libraries Unlimited, 2011.

Stakhov, A. P., and Scott Anthony Olsen. *The Mathematics of Harmony: From Euclid to Contemporary Mathematics and Computer Science.* Hackensack, NJ: World Scientific, 2009.

Taylor, Arlene G., and Daniel N. Joudrey. *The Organization of Information.* 3rd ed. Westport, CT: Libraries Unlimited, 2009.

Valacich, Joseph S., Christoph Schneider, and Leonard M. Jessup. *Information Systems Today: Managing in the Digital World*. 7th ed. Boston, MA: Pearson, 2016.

INDEX

P

Q

R

S